1stClassEconomics.com

Econometrics
Revision Notes

Bahrum Lamehdasht

1stClassEconomics.com

© Bahrum Lamehdasht 2012

All rights reserved. No part of this publication may be reproduced, stored in a retrieval system or transmitted in any form or by any means, electronic, mechanical or photocopying, recording, or otherwise without prior permission of the publisher.

Contents

Ordinary Least Squares	pp.1-2
Normality	pp.5-6
Inference Tests	pp.7-10
Modelling	pp.11-13
Model Specification Tests	pp.14-15
Multicollinearity	pp.16-20
Heteroskedasticity	pp.21-28
Autocorrelation	pp.29-35
Koyck Transformation	pp.36-37
Spurious Regression	p.38
Time Stationarity	pp.39-41
Unit Root Tests	pp.42-43
Cointegration	p.44
Cointegration Tests	pp.45-46
Error Correction Models	pp.47-48
Estimating Error Correction Models	pp.49-50
Panel Data	pp.51-55
Instrumental Variables	pp.56-59
Logit and Probit Models	pp.60-65
Sample Selection Bias	pp.66-69
Appendix A	pp.70-76

Ordinary Least Squares

Ordinary Least Squares (OLS)[1]

Ordinary Least Squares (OLS) is a regression technique to estimate a linear relationship between two or more variables. Let's say we have the population regression function (PRF):

$$Y_i = \beta_1 + \beta_2 X_i + u_i$$

The PRF shows the true relationship between the variables. A PRF measures how the average of Y responds to a change in X. Based on a sample of the population, OLS estimates the sample regression function (SRF):

$$Y_i = \hat{\beta}_1 + \hat{\beta}_2 X_i + \hat{u}_i$$

OLS: PRF and SRF

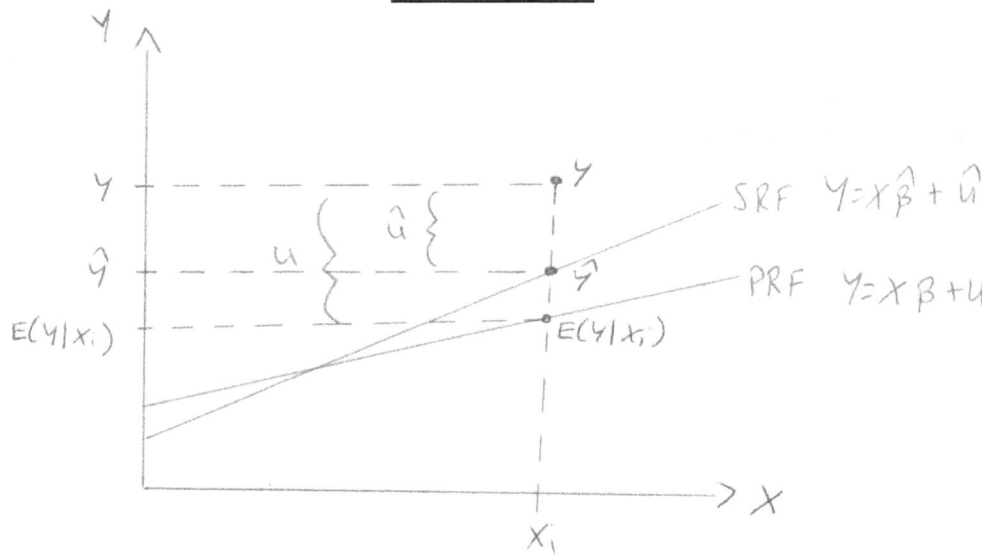

The SRF approximates the PRF. OLS estimates the PRF by minimizing the residual sum of squares (RSS). By minimizing RSS, OLS equally weights both positive and negative residuals. OLS minimizes an absolute value of the residuals and therefore approximates the SRF as close as possible to the PRF.

$$Y_i = \hat{Y}_i + \hat{u}_i$$

$$\hat{u}_i = Y_i - \hat{Y}_i$$

$$RSS = \sum \hat{u}_i^2 = \sum (Y_i - \hat{Y}_i)^2$$

---

[1] See Appendix A for OLS in matrix form.

1stClassEconomics.com

Classical Linear Regression Model (CLRM)
OLS relies on the assumptions of the Classical Linear Regression Model (CLRM):

Assumptions of the Regressors (X):
A.1) X is nonstochastic, it takes values determined by the researcher.
A.2) X is fixed in repeated sampling.
A.3) As the sample size (n) approaches ∞, Var(X) is finite and constant.
A.4) No perfect multicollinearity, otherwise we cannot estimate the regressors' separate effects on the dependent variable.

Assumptions of the Residuals (u):
B.1) The expected value of the residuals equals zero, that is, E(u_i) = 0, so the random error term does not systematically affect the mean of Y.
B.2) $Var(u_i) = E(u_i u_i') = \sigma^2$, there is homoskedastic variance of u. So all Y are equally important, equally reliable and deviate from their mean by the same extent.
B.3) No autocorrelation, $Cov(u_i, u_j) = E\left((u_i - E(u_i))(u_j - E(u_j))\right) = E(u_i u_j) = 0$ for $i \neq j$.

Additional Assumptions:
C.1) Correct model specification, for example, no omitted variables bias.
C.2) The sample size n is greater than the number of parameters k.
C.3) The regression model is linear in parameters, for example, β not β^2.

The Normal Equations
OLS estimates $\hat{\beta}$ by minimizing the RSS and then partially differentiating it by $\hat{\beta}$.

$$RSS = \sum \hat{u}_i^2 = \sum (Y_i - \hat{Y}_i)^2 = \sum (Y_i - \hat{\beta}_1 + \hat{\beta}_2 X_i)^2$$

$$\frac{\delta \sum \hat{u}_i^2}{\delta \hat{\beta}_1} = -2 \sum (Y_i - \hat{\beta}_1 + \hat{\beta}_2 X_i) = -2 \sum \hat{u}_i$$

$$0 = -2 \sum (Y_i - \hat{\beta}_1 + \hat{\beta}_2 X_i) = \sum (Y_i - \hat{\beta}_1 + \hat{\beta}_2 X_i) = \sum Y_i - n\hat{\beta}_1 - \hat{\beta}_2 \sum X_i$$

And thus the first normal equation is:

$$\sum Y_i = n\hat{\beta}_1 + \hat{\beta}_2 \sum X_i$$

To derive the second normal equation:

$$\frac{\delta \sum \hat{u}_i^2}{\delta \hat{\beta}_1} = -2 X_i \sum (Y_i - \hat{\beta}_1 + \hat{\beta}_2 X_i) = -2 \sum \hat{u}_i X_i$$

$$0 = -2 \sum X_i \sum (Y_i - \hat{\beta}_1 + \hat{\beta}_2 X_i) = \sum Y_i X_i - \hat{\beta}_1 \sum X_i - \hat{\beta}_2 \sum X_i^2$$

And thus the second normal equation is:

$$\sum Y_i X_i = \hat{\beta}_1 \sum X_i + \hat{\beta}_2 \sum X_i^2$$

Best Linear Unbiased Estimator (BLUE)

Assuming the Gauss-Markov conditions (A.1) X is nonstochastic, (A.2) X is fixed in repeated sampling, (B.1) $E(u_i) = 0$, (B.2) no heteroskedasticity and (B.3) no autocorrelation then the OLS estimators are best linear unbiased estimators (BLUE) in small samples.

Linear

An estimator $\hat{\theta}$ is a linear estimate of the true population value θ if it is a linear function of the sample observations. $\hat{\beta}$ is linear because it is a linear function of the sample observations Y.

Best and Unbiased

$\hat{\beta}$ is best because it has minimum variance amongst all other linear estimators.

$\hat{\beta}$ is unbiased since $E(\hat{\beta}) = \beta$

Best and Unbiased

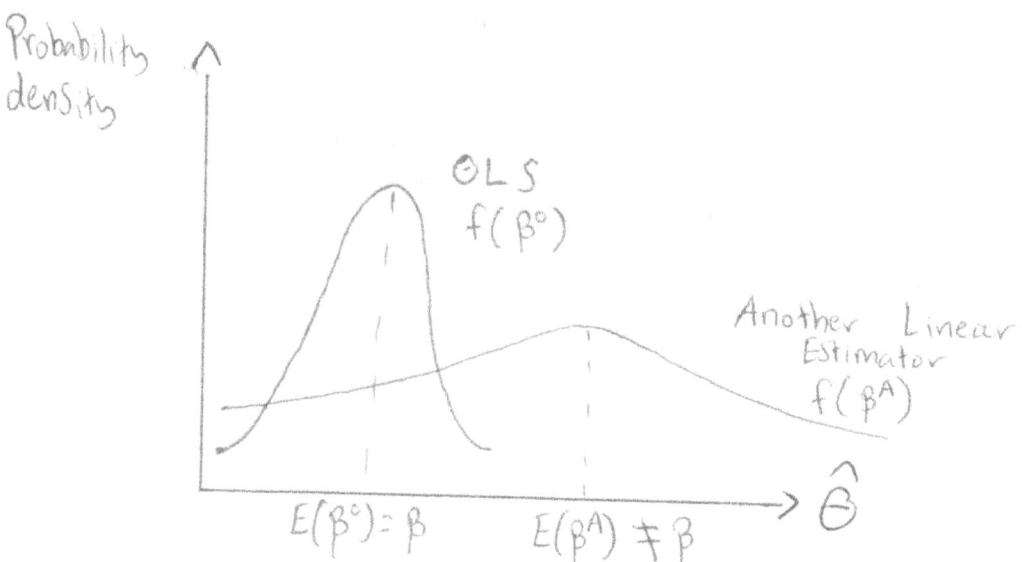

Proof of $\hat{\beta}$ Unbiasedness

Let's look at the OLS equation for the slope coefficient $\hat{\beta}_2$:

$$\hat{\beta}_2 = \frac{\sum x_i Y_i}{\sum x_i^2}$$

Where $x_i = (X_i - \bar{X})$.

Define a constant:

$$k_i = \frac{x_i}{\left(\sum x_i^2\right)}$$

And this constant k_i has the following properties:
- k_i is nonstochastic as it is a function of X_i.
- $\sum k_i = 0$ as $\sum k_i = \sum \frac{1}{\sum x_i^2} \cdot \sum x_i$ where $\sum x_i = 0$.
- $\sum k_i^2 = \frac{1}{\sum x_i^2}$.
- $\sum k_i x_i$.

Substituting the PRF into the OLS equation for $\hat{\beta}_2$:

$$\hat{\beta}_2 = \frac{\sum x_i Y_i}{\sum x_i^2} = \sum k_i Y_i = \sum k_i (\beta_1 + \beta_2 X_i + u_i) = \beta_1 \sum k_i + \beta_2 \sum k_i X_i + \sum k_i u_i$$
$$= \beta_2 + \sum k_i u_i$$

And now:

$$E(\hat{\beta}_2) = E(\beta_2) + E\left(\sum k_i u_i\right) = E(\beta_2) + \sum k_i E(u_i) = \beta_2$$

Normality

Another assumption we must make for regression analysis is normality. We must assume the residual is normally distributed $u_i \sim N(0, \sigma^2)$. Normality is not one of the Classical Linear Regression Model assumptions and it is not required for OLS to be BLUE. Normality is required for inferential statements, like t tests, to be correct.

Normality

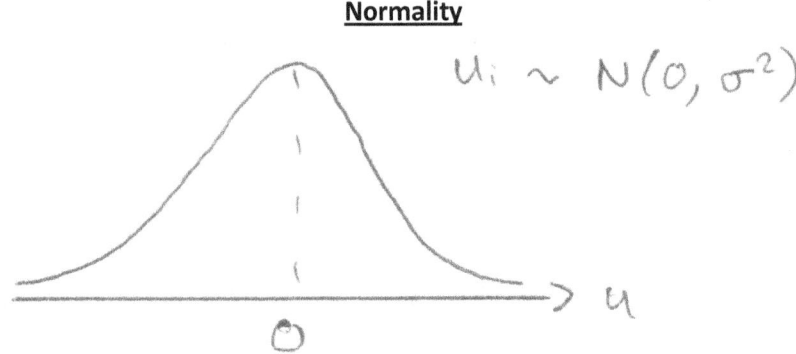

The Residual or Error Term

Let's look at a simple linear regression model:

$$y_i = \beta_1 + \beta_2 X_i + u_i$$

The residual u_i reflects the variation in y_i that is unexplained by X_i.

There is unexplained variation because:
- We simply may not know all the explanatory factors of Δy_i.
- Unavailable data may force us to omit some regressors.
- Some regressors may be too costly to acquire data for.
- Occam's razor influences us to keep a simple model that explains a lot.
- We may be using the wrong functional form.
- Intrinsic randomness in human behaviour.

Normality Assumption

In regression analysis we want to estimate a sample regression function and then use it to make inferences about the population regression function. And since $\hat{\beta}$ are random variables, we must find out their probability distributions to relate them to their true population values.

$$\hat{\beta}_2 = \sum k_i (\beta_1 + \beta_2 X_i + u_i)$$

Where $k_i = \frac{x_i}{\sum x_i^2}$.

Because k_i, βs and X_i are all fixed, $\hat{\beta}$ is a linear function of u_i. So the probability distribution of $\hat{\beta}$ depends on the probability distribution of u_i. Because of the Central Limit Theorem (CLT), we assume u_i is asymptotically normally distributed. The CLT states: As the sample size → ∞, probability distributions → the normal distribution.

As a result, if the residual is normally distributed $u_i \sim N(0, \sigma^2)$ then $\hat{\beta} \sim N(\beta, \sigma_{\hat{\beta}}^2)$ so:

$$Z = \frac{\hat{\beta} - \beta}{s.e.(\hat{\beta})} = \frac{(\hat{\beta} - \beta)\sqrt{X_i^2}}{\sigma}$$

Or, if we have to estimate σ then:

$$t = \frac{\hat{\beta} - \beta}{\hat{\sigma}} = \frac{(\hat{\beta} - \beta)\sqrt{X_i^2}}{\hat{\sigma}}$$

And now we can use hypothesis tests to make inferences about $\hat{\beta}$.

Jarque-Bera Test of Normality

A test of normality is the Jarque-Bera (JB) test.

$$Skewness\ S = \frac{E(X_i - \bar{X})}{\sigma^3} = \frac{\frac{1}{n}\sum(X_i - \bar{X})}{\sigma^3}$$

$$Kurtosis\ K = \frac{E(X_i - \bar{X})^4}{(E(X_i - \bar{X})^2)^2} = \frac{\frac{1}{n}\sum(X_i - \bar{X})^4}{\sigma^4}$$

Null hypothesis $H_o: S = 0\ and\ K = 3\ so\ u_i \sim N(0, \sigma^2)$ and there is normality.

Alternative hypothesis H_1: At least one of the S and K normality conditions do not hold.

JB test stat:

$$JB = n\left[\frac{S^2}{6} + \frac{(K-3)^3}{24}\right] \sim X_2^2$$

If the JB stat is greater than the chi-square critical value at the chosen level of significance then reject the null hypothesis, u_i is not normally distributed. If the JB stat is less than the chi-square critical value at the chosen level of significance then do not reject the null hypothesis, u_i is normally distributed.

Inference Tests

t test

A t test is a test of individual statistical significance using sample results to verify the truth or falsity of a null hypothesis[2].

Let's say we have the regression model:

$$y_i = \beta_0 + \beta_1 X_{1i} + \beta_2 X_{2i} + u_i$$

The t statistic is:

$$t\,stat = \frac{\widehat{\beta_2} - \beta_2^{null}}{s.e.(\widehat{\beta_2})} \sim t(\alpha, n-k)$$

Where t(n-k) is the t critical value obtained from the t table, α is the level of significance, n is the sample size and k is the number of parameters β including the intercept.

And our hypotheses are:

$$Null\ hypothesis\ H_o: \beta_2 = 0$$

$$Alternative\ hypothesis\ H_1: \beta_2 \neq 0$$

t test

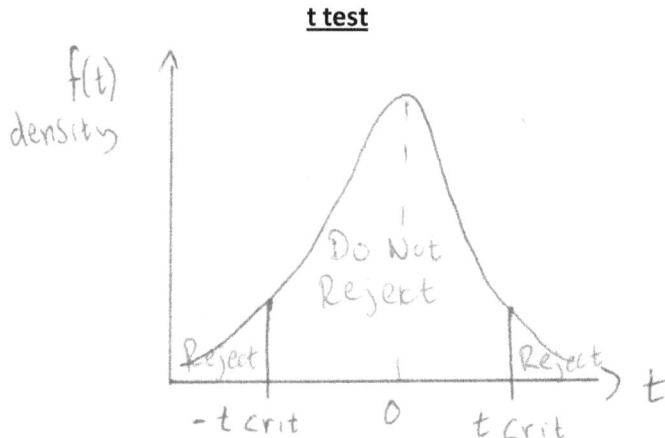

If the t stat > t critical value (α, df), reject the null hypothesis, the variable is statistically significant at the α% level of significance.

Alternatively, if the t stat < t critical value (α, df), do not reject the null hypothesis[3], the variable is statistically insignificant at the α% level of significance.

---

[2] All we are doing with a t test is testing if one of our βs is significant, if it is then the corresponding X has an effect on y, if it is not then the corresponding X has no effect on y.

[3] Note that we do not say "accept the null hypothesis" for this is technically not true. All we can be sure is that we do not reject the null hypothesis, we do not know for sure whether we accept it or not.

Type 1 and Type 2 Errors
A type 1 error is $\alpha\%$, the % chance of rejecting a true null hypothesis.
A type 2 error is the % chance of accepting a false null hypothesis.

As the % chance of making a type 1 error falls, the % chance of making a type 2 error must rise.

And 1 minus the type 2 error equals the 'power of the test' to reject a false null hypothesis.

P-Value
A p-value is the lowest level of significance at which we can reject the null hypothesis[4]. It is also the exact % chance of making a type 1 error.

F-Test
An F-test is a test of joint statistical significance[5].

Let's say we have the regression model:

$$y_i = \beta_0 + \beta_1 X_{1i} + \beta_2 X_{2i} + \cdots + \beta_k X_{ki} + u_i$$

And our hypotheses are:

$$Null\ hypothesis\ H_o: \beta_1 = \beta_2 = \cdots = \beta_k = 0$$

$$Alternative\ hypothesis\ H_1: At\ least\ one\ slope\ coefficient \neq 0$$

The F statistic is:

$$F\ stat = \frac{R^2/(k-1)}{(1-R^2)/(n-k)} \sim F(\alpha, ((k-1), (n-k)))$$

If the F stat > F critical value, reject the null hypothesis, the model is jointly significant in explaining the variation in y (or alternatively put, the model possesses some degree of explanatory power) at the $\alpha\%$ level of significance.

If the F stat < F critical value, do not reject the null hypothesis, the model is jointly insignificant in explaining the variation in y (or alternatively put, the model possesses no explanatory power) at the $\alpha\%$ level of significance.

---

[4] P-values are the easiest way of conducting t tests. Let's say the p-value of an estimate $\hat{\beta}$ is 0.05 or 5%. Without having to calculate anything we know that we can reject the null hypothesis at the 5% level and any level higher (for example, 10% or 20%) but no level lower (for example, 1% or 3%).
[5] All we are doing is testing to see whether all of our regressors act together to have an effect on y.

1stClassEconomics.com

R Squared (R^2)

R^2 is a measure of goodness of fit, it measures the % of the variation in Y explained by the model.

Given the sample regression function:

$$y_i = \hat{y}_i + \hat{u}_i$$
$$y_i - \bar{y} = \hat{y}_i - \bar{y} + \hat{u}_i$$

$$(y_i - \bar{y})^2 = (\hat{y}_i - \bar{y} + \hat{u}_i)^2$$

$$(y_i - \bar{y})^2 = (\hat{y}_i - \bar{y})^2 + \hat{u}_i^2 + 2(\hat{y}_i - \bar{y})\hat{u}_i$$

$$\sum(y_i - \bar{y})^2 = \sum(\hat{y}_i - \bar{y})^2 + \sum \hat{u}_i^2 + 2\sum(\hat{y}_i - \bar{y})\hat{u}_i$$

And since $\sum(\hat{y}_i - \bar{y})\hat{u}_i = 0$ then:

$$\sum(y_i - \bar{y})^2 = \sum(\hat{y}_i - \bar{y})^2 + \sum \hat{u}_i^2$$

$$Total\ Sum\ of\ Squares\ (TSS)$$
$$= Explained\ Sum\ of\ Squares\ (ESS) + Residual\ Sum\ of\ Squares\ (RSS)$$

$$R^2 = \frac{ESS}{TSS} = \frac{TSS - RSS}{TSS} = 1 - \frac{RSS}{TSS}$$

As $ESS \to 0$, $R^2 \to 0$ and the model has less explanatory power.
As $RSS \to 0$, $R^2 \to 1$ and the model has more explanatory power.

If, for example, $R^2 = 0.997$, then the model explains 99.7% of the variation in y.

Comparing Models Using R^2

When using R^2 to choose between which regression model has the most explanatory power, beware of the following:

1) R^2 can only be used to compare models if y is the same.

2) The data frequency must be the same between the models, for example, one model cannot be using quarterly data whilst another model uses annual data.

3) R^2 has no causal relationship, it just shows correlation.

4) Because the conventional R^2 formula assumes an intercept, if there is no intercept in the model then R^2 could be negative.

5) A high R^2 does not necessarily mean the model characterizes the data well. A sample regression function could fit many different versions of data.

6) R^2 cannot be used to judge between models with different amounts of regressors because R^2 gives an unfair advantage to models with more regressors. Adding a regressor generally increases R^2 since the regressor usually has some degree of explanatory power. Instead, we

must use the adjusted R squared $\bar{R}^2$ since this uses degrees of freedom as a penalty for adding regressors.

$$\bar{R}^2 = 1 - \frac{\frac{RSS}{n-k}}{\frac{TSS}{n-1}} = 1 - R^2\frac{(n-1)}{(n-k)}$$

Adding another X causes RSS to fall, so $\bar{R}^2$ rises. But also, k rises, (n-k) falls so $\frac{\frac{RSS}{n-k}}{\frac{TSS}{n-1}}$ rises and $\bar{R}^2$ falls.

$\bar{R}^2$ may rise or fall when another regressor is added.

7) Do not base a model's plausibility entirely on its R^2. A model should be based more on economic theory. Adding/dropping regressors to maximize R^2 is a form of 'data mining' and basically renders the model useless.

Modelling

Omitted Variable Bias

By omitting a relevant regressor we get omitted variable bias (OVB) and OLS is no longer BLUE because our $\hat{\beta}$ coefficients become biased. Also Var($\hat{\beta}$) usually falls.

Let's say the 'true' or BLUE model is:

$$y = \beta_1 + \beta_2 X_2 + \beta_3 X_3 + u$$

And the misspecified model with the omitted regressor is:

$$\hat{y} = b_1 + b_2 X_2$$

The b_2 slope coefficient is estimated by:

$$b_2 = \frac{Cov(X_2, y)}{Var(X_2)} = \frac{Cov(X_2, (\beta_1 + \beta_2 X_2 + \beta_3 X_3 + u))}{Var(X_2)}$$

$$= \frac{Cov(X_2, \beta_1) + Cov(X_2, \beta_2 X_2) + Cov(X_2, \beta_3 X_3) + Cov(X_2, u)}{Var(X_2)}$$

$$= \frac{0 + \beta_2 Cov(X_2, X_3) + \beta_3 Cov(X_2, X_3) + Cov(X_2, u)}{Var(X_2)}$$

$$= \beta_2 + \beta_3 \frac{Cov(X_2, X_3)}{Var(X_2)} + \frac{Cov(X_2, u)}{Var(X_2)}$$

$$E(b_2) = E(\beta_2) + E\left(\beta_3 \frac{Cov(X_2, X_3)}{Var(X_2)}\right) + E\left(\frac{Cov(X_2, u)}{Var(X_2)}\right)$$

And since $Cov(X_2, u) = 0$ (a CLRM assumption) we get:

$$E(b_2) = \beta_2 + \beta_3 \frac{Cov(X_2, X_3)}{Var(X_2)}$$

Where β_2 is the true parameter value, β_3 is included in the BLUE model so it must be statistically $\neq 0$ and $\frac{Cov(X_2, X_3)}{Var(X_2)} \neq 0$ as there is likely to be some degree of multicollinearity between X_2 and X_3.

So the estimator b_2 is biased by the amount $\beta_3 \frac{Cov(X_2, X_3)}{Var(X_2)}$.

If $\beta_3 > 0$ then b_2 is upward biased as it captures the positive explanatory power of β_3.

And if $\beta_3 < 0$ then b_2 is downward biased as it captures the negative explanatory power of β_3.

Because:

$$Var(b_2) = \frac{RSS/(n-k)}{\sum x_{2i}^2}$$

And:

$$Var(\hat{\beta}_2) = \frac{RSS/(n-k)}{\sum x_{2i}^2 (1 - r_{23}^2)}$$

If there is some degree of multicollinearity between X_2 and X_3, $r_{23} \neq 0$, $Var(\hat{\beta}_2) > Var(b_2)$. So $Var(b_2)$ is downward biased. This invalidates our t tests because our t stat falls[6] as it depends negatively on $\sqrt{Var(b_2)}$.

Adding Irrelevant Regressors
By adding an irrelevant regressor, our $\hat{\beta}$ slope coefficients are still unbiased but $Var(b)$ rises.

Let's say the 'true' or BLUE model is:

$$y = \beta_1 + \beta_2 X_2 + u$$

And the misspecified model with the irrelevant regressor is:

$$\hat{y} = b_1 + b_2 X_2 + b_3 X_3$$

The expected value of the b_2 slope coefficient is:

$$E(b_2) = \beta_2 + \beta_3 \frac{Cov(X_2, X_3)}{Var(X_2)}$$

Because X_3 is not in the BLUE model, β_3 is insignificant and equal to zero so there is no bias. But:

$$Var(b_2) = \frac{\sigma^2}{\sum x_{2i}^2 (1 - r_{23}^2)}$$

And:

$$Var(\hat{\beta}_2) = \frac{\sigma^2}{\sum x_{2i}^2}$$

So, if X_2 and X_3 have some degree of multicollinearity then adding X_3 to our model will make r_{23}^2 rise, increase $Var(b_2)$ so that $Var(b_2) > Var(\hat{\beta}_2)$ and therefore invalidate our t tests because our t stat rises[7] as it depends negatively on $\sqrt{Var(b_2)}$.

---
[6] So our t tests will wrongly conclude that our estimates are more significant than they actually are in the BLUE model.

Dummy Variables

A dummy variable lets us add qualitative variables by classifying data into mutually exclusive categories.

Let's say we have the regression model with a dummy variable as the regressor:

$$y_i = \beta_0 + \beta_1 d_{1i} + u_i$$

d=1 means the dummy is switched on and the average of y_i is $\beta_0 + \beta_1$. d=0 means the dummy is switched off, the 'benchmark category', and the average of y_i is β_0.

But, we must be careful to avoid the dummy trap. M categories and M dummies causes perfect multicollinearity. To avoid the dummy trap we must use no more than M-1 dummies or do not include an intercept.

Data Mining

A researcher may build a model by adding/dropping regressors until it is significant at some pre-specified level of significance. This is called 'data mining' and it is wrong to do it. A model should be made by economic theory and then its significance should be interpreted. A researcher should not go 'looking for an answer' that is not there by building a model to make sure a variable is significant/insignificant.

Data mining changes the level of significance to:

$$\alpha^* = 1 - (1 - \alpha)^{c/k}$$

Where c is number of parameters at the start of data mining, k is the number of parameters at the end of data mining, α is the level of significance at the start of data mining and α^* is the level of significance after data mining.

---

[7] So our t tests will wrongly conclude that our estimates are less significant than they actually are in the BLUE model.

Model Specification Tests

Ramsey RESET Test

The Ramsey RESET test is a test of general misspecification of functional form. Ramsey RESET is an easy test to apply because you do not need to know what the misspecification is.

Let's say we have a regression model:

$$y_i = \lambda_1 + \lambda_2 X_i + u_i$$

Rationale of Ramsey RESET: Say we regress the above regression model and plot the residuals against the regressand and a pattern emerges. This would make us suspect that we have omitted some nonlinear form of X from our model. So by adding some higher power quadratics of $\hat{y}_i$ into the model, the R^2 should rise. If the rise in R^2 is statistically significant then we have model misspecification.

Ramsey RESET follows these steps:

1) Regress:

$$y_i = \lambda_1 + \lambda_2 X_i + u_i$$

   Obtain $\hat{y}_i$ and R_{old}^2.

2) Add higher order $\hat{y}_i$ values and regress:

$$y_i = \beta_1 + \beta_2 X_i + \beta_3 \hat{y}_i^2 + \beta_4 \hat{y}_i^3 + u_i$$

   And obtain R_{new}^2.

3) $F\ stat = \dfrac{\frac{R_{new}^2 - R_{old}^2}{a}}{\frac{1 - R_{new}^2}{n-k}} \sim F(q, (n-k))$

   Where a is the number of new regressors and n-k is for the new model.

4) $H_o : Correct\ Model\ Specification$

   $H_1 : Model\ Misspecification$

5) If the F stat > F critical value at the chosen level of significance then reject the null hypothesis, there is some sort of functional form problem.

   If the F stat < F critical value at the chosen level of significance then do not reject the null hypothesis, there is correct model specification.

But:
- How many functions of $\hat{y}_i$ should be added in step 2? Maybe $\hat{y}_i^2$ and $\hat{y}_i^3$ are enough.

- Ramsey RESET is a test for general misspecification, it does not tell us exactly what the misspecification is.

Residuals
A simple model specification test is to plot the residuals (maybe against a regressor, the regressand, time or their own lagged values) and check for patterns.

Chow Test
The Chow test is a test of structural stability. A time series regression may have a structural break at some point where the coefficients change after a certain period of time. For example, let's say we have the following model with the following sub-periods:

$$\text{Pooled model: } y_t = \beta_1 + \beta_2 X_t + u_t \quad \text{N observations}$$
$$\text{Model for sub-period A: } y_t = \alpha_1 + \alpha_2 X_t + u_{tA} \quad \text{NA observations}$$
$$\text{Model for sub-period B: } y_t = \gamma_1 + \gamma_2 X_t + u_{tB} \quad \text{NB observations}$$

The Chow test then has the following steps:

1) Estimate the pooled model and obtain RSS_R, degrees of freedom (N-k) and degrees of freedom k.

2) Estimate the sub-period A model and obtain RSS_A and degrees of freedom (NA-k).

3) Estimate the sub-period B model and obtain RSS_B and degrees of freedom (NB-k).

4) $RSS_{UR} = RSS_A + RSS_B$.

5) F stat = $\frac{(RSS_R - RSS_{UR})/k}{RSS_{UR}/(N-2k)} \sim F(k, (N-2k))$.

6) H_o: Structural stability, all coefficients are the same between sub-period A and sub-period B.

   H_1: Structural break, at least one coefficient is different between sub-period A and sub-period B.

7) If the F stat > F critical value then reject the null hypothesis at the chosen level of significance, a structural break is present.

   If the F stat < F critical value then do not reject the null hypothesis at the chosen level of significance, there is structural stability.

But:
- The residuals for the sub-period regression models must be normally distributed with no heteroskedasticity or autocorrelation.
- Assumes we know when the structural break occurs … do we?
- Does not tell us if the slope, intercept or both break. But the dummy approach to structural breaks does.

Multicollinearity

Multicollinearity (MC): Definition
Multicollinearity (MC)[8] occurs when the sample values of regressors are highly correlated. With perfect MC there is an exact linear relationship between the sample values of our regressors. With imperfect MC there is an approximate linear relationship between the sample values of our regressors.

Perfect MC	Imperfect MC
All of the variation in Y explained by X_3 is also fully explained by X_2.	Some of the variation in Y is explained by both X_3 and X_2.

It becomes difficult to disentangle the separate effects of the regressors on Y.

Causalities
MC may be caused by numerous factors including:

1) Time series where variables share a common trend, for example:

$$Consumption = \beta_0 + \beta_1 Income + \beta_3 Wealth + u$$

Income and wealth both rise at similar rates over time and exert similar effects on consumption.

2) Model specification error, an over-determined model, maybe too many similar regressors are in the model.

3) Micronumerosity. Goldberger's term for when the sample size (n) is just about greater than the number of parameters (k). A small sample size makes the regressors look correlated when, in larger samples, they are not. The problem here is not enough data to show the variation in the regressors.

Consequences
Perfect MC and imperfect MC have different consequences.

Perfect MC
If there is perfect MC then OLS cannot even estimate our βs.

---

[8] See Appendix A for matrix notation of perfect and imperfect MC.

Let's say:

$$X_{3i} = \lambda X_{2i}$$

And as X_{2i} increases by 1 unit, X_{3i} increases by λ. So the separate effects of X_{2i} and X_{2i} on the dependent variable cannot be estimated.

$$y_i = \hat{\beta}_2 x_{2i} + \hat{\beta}_3 x_{3i} + u_i$$

$$\hat{\beta}_2 = \frac{(\sum y_i x_{2i})(\sum x_{3i}^2) - (\sum y_i x_{3i})(\sum x_{2i} x_{3i})}{(\sum x_{2i}^2)(\sum x_{3i}^2) - (\sum x_{2i} x_{3i})^2}$$

$$\hat{\beta}_2 = \frac{(\sum y_i x_{2i})(\lambda^2 \sum x_{2i}^2) - (\lambda \sum y_i x_{2i})(\lambda \sum x_{2i}^2)}{(\sum x_{2i}^2)(\lambda^2 \sum x_{2i}^2) - \lambda^2 (\sum x_{2i}^2)^2} = \frac{0}{0} = 0$$

So OLS estimation of $\hat{\beta}$ is impossible.

Imperfect MC

If there is imperfect multicollinearity then the Var($\hat{\beta}$) and s.e.($\hat{\beta}$) become large and our inferential tests become invalid. Although, it must be noted that OLS remains BLUE if there is imperfect MC (so long as the other Gauss-Markov conditions hold).

$$Var(\hat{\beta}_j) = \frac{\sigma^2}{\sum x_j^2} \cdot VIF$$

$$VIF = \frac{1}{(1 - R_j^2)}$$

Where R_j^2 is from an auxiliary regression of x_j on all the other regressors. VIF measures the speed of the increase in $Var(\hat{\beta}_j)$ as R_j^2.

With no MC, $R_j^2 = 0$, VIF = 1 and:

$$Var(\hat{\beta}_j) = \frac{\sigma^2}{\sum x_j^2}.$$

As MC increases, R_j^2 increases, VIF increases and $Var(\hat{\beta}_j)$ increases.

Because $= \frac{\hat{\beta}_j - \beta_{null}}{s.e.(\hat{\beta})}$, as MC increases, our regressors become even more correlated, s.e.($\hat{\beta}$) rises, the t stat falls and becomes less significant. There is an increased chance of making a type 2 error (accepting a false null hypothesis). Because our t stats are invalidated, we may conclude that the $\hat{\beta}s$ are individually insignificant even though they are collectively significant because of a high R^2.

Multicollinearity: Confidence Intervals

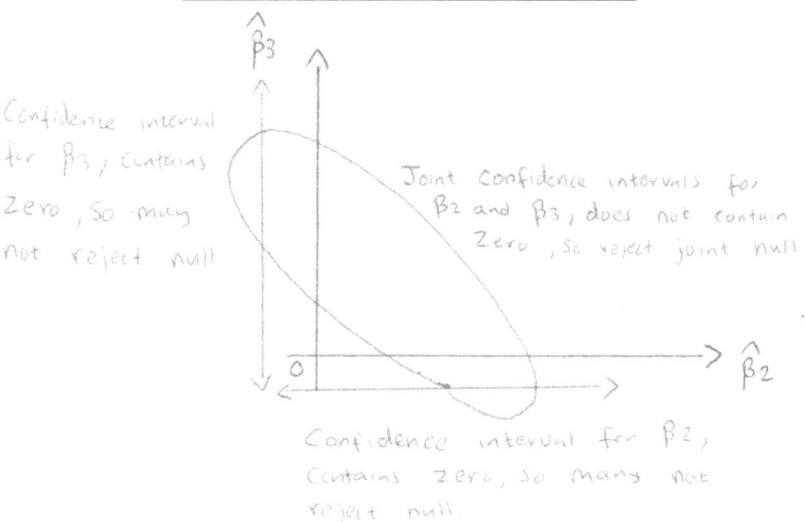

Additionally, our OLS estimators become imprecise and both the OLS estimators and standard errors become sensitive to small changes in the data.

Detection
MC may be detected by various methods:

1) A high R^2 and many insignificant t stats could indicate MC. Although, this may just be coincidence.

2) Eigenvalues.
$$k = \frac{Maximum\ eigenvalue}{Minimum\ eigenvalue}$$

   If $100 \leq k \leq 1000$ then there is moderate MC. If $k > 1000$ then there is serious MC.

3) Variance inflating factor (VIF).

VIF

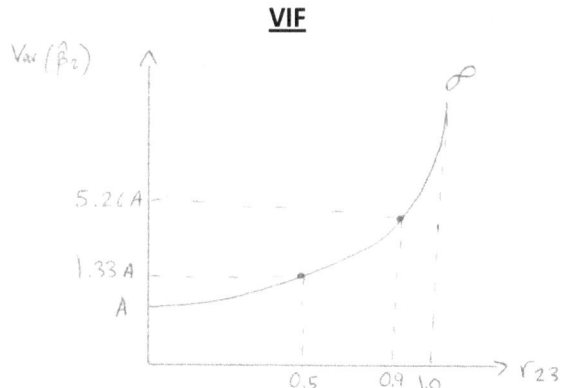

Where $A = \frac{\sigma^2}{\sum x_{2i}^2}$ and r_{23} is the correlation coefficient between x_2 and x_3.

MC becomes a problem when $r_{23} > 0.9$ or conversely when VIF > 5.26. But, this is only a sufficient condition, it is not a necessary condition because there could still be MC even if VIF does not indicate MC.

4) Auxiliary regression of an X on all the other Xs could be run and then the F test can be used to detect the presence of MC.

Auxiliary regression steps:
- The null hypothesis $H_o: no\ MC$ and alternative hypothesis $H_1: MC$.
- Regress X_1 on all the other regressors $X_2, X_3 \ldots X_k$ and obtain R_A^2.
- F stat = $\frac{R_A^2/(k-2)}{(1-R_A^2)/(n-k+1)}$, where k is the number of parameters.

If the F stat > F critical value at the chosen level of significance then that particular X is collinear with other Xs and we reject the null hypothesis of no MC.

But, many auxiliary regressions need to be run and this method does not reveal exactly which Xs are correlated, just that one or more are correlated.

Remedies
Many remedies can be used to cure MC including:

1) Maybe MC is a problem with that particular sample being used, so you could just use a different sample.

2) Do nothing. Because:

   - MC may exist but may be a negligible problem.
   - MC may be a data deficiency problem, micronumerosity, and sometimes we have no choice over the available data.
   - Many low insignificant t stats and a high R^2 does not necessarily reveal MC, it could be coincidence, it could be the actual relationship between the variables.
   - If R^2 is high and prediction is seeked then MC is not a problem. Although, interpretation will be difficult.

3) Drop the regressor(s) suffering MC. But, this could lead to omitted variables bias (OVB) and worsen the problem since OVB makes OLS not BLUE whilst OLS is still BLUE under MC.

4) First-difference the variables. Variables may be correlated over time but there is no reason why their differences should be correlated over time. Assuming the regression model holds in all time periods:

(A) $Y_t = \beta_1 + \beta_2 X_{2t} + \beta_3 X_{3t} + u_t$

(B) $Y_{t-1} = \beta_1 + \beta_2 X_{2t-1} + \beta_3 X_{3t-1} + u_{t-1}$

(A) Minus (B) $Y_t - Y_{t-1} = \beta_2(X_{2t} - X_{2t-1}) + \beta_3(X_{3t} - X_{3t-1}) + (u_t - u_{t-1})$

This gives us:

$$\Delta Y_t = \beta_2 \Delta X_{2t} + \beta_3 \Delta X_{3t} + \Delta u_t$$

MC should now disappear. But, this could cause autocorrelation.

5) A prior expectation to combine variables. If we have:

$$Y_i = \beta_0 + \beta_1 X_{1i} + \beta_2 X_{2i} + u_i$$

And we know that $\beta_2 = 0.10\beta_1$ then:

$$Y_i = \beta_0 + \beta_1 X_i + u_i$$

Where $X_i = X_{1i} + 0.10 X_{2i}$.

After we obtain $\hat{\beta}_1$ we can obtain $\hat{\beta}_2$ from $\beta_2 = 0.10\beta_1$.

6) Because:

$$Var(\hat{\beta}_i) = \frac{\sigma_u^2}{\sum x_j^2 (1 - R_j^2)}$$

To dampen the effect of MC we could:
- Include more relevant variables to decrease σ_u^2. But, we could over-fit the model and increase MC.
- Add new data to increase the sample size (n) and increase $\sum x_j^2$. But, is new data available?
- Increase $Var(X_j)$. But, this is only an option during the model design stage.

Heteroskedasticity

Heteroskedasticity (HK) Definition
Heteroskedasticity (HK)[9] occurs when the variance of the error term is non-constant $E(u_i^2)$.

Homoskedasticity
$$Var(u_i) = \sigma^2$$
same for every i

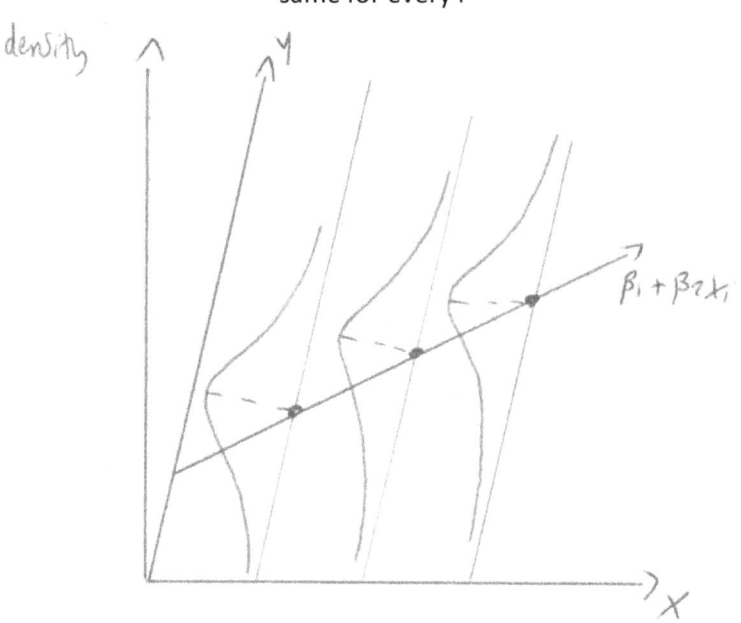

Heteroskedasticity
$$Var(u_i) = \sigma_i^2$$
different for every i

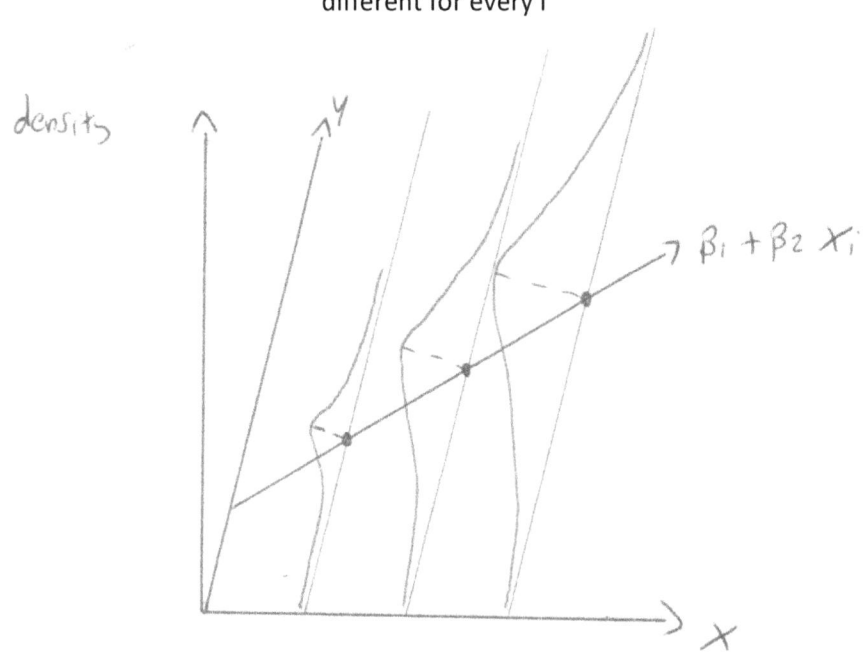

---

[9] See Appendix A for the matrix notation of HK consequences.

Causalities
Many factors could cause HK including:

1) In error-learning models, as people learn their errors decrease and σ_i^2 falls over time.

2) As incomes rise, people have more discretionary income, more choice over the scope of the disposition of their income and thus σ_i^2 increases.

3) As data collection techniques improve, errors fall and σ_i^2 falls.

4) An outlier (an observation from a different population) could make σ_i^2 rise or fall.

5) Skewness in the distribution of regressors could make σ_i^2 rise or fall.

6) Model misspecification. Omitted variable bias means the residuals soak up the missing explanatory power and the residuals then appear more (less) dispersed around its mean so σ_i^2 may rise (fall).

Consequences
HK infects the variances of OLS estimates, OLS is no longer BLUE. Weighted Least Squares (WLS[10]) estimates are BLUE when HK is present.

Let's look at the OLS variance of $\hat{\beta}$:

$$Var(\hat{\beta}_1)_{OLS} = \frac{\sigma^2}{(\sum x_i^2)}$$

And the variance of $\hat{\beta}$ when OLS accounts for HK:

$$Var(\hat{\beta}_1)_{HK} = \frac{\sum x_i^2 \sigma_i^2}{(\sum x_i^2)}$$

And the WLS variance of $\hat{\beta}$:

$$Var(\hat{\beta}_1)_{WLS} = \frac{\sum W_i}{(\sum W_i)(\sum W_i X_i^2) - (\sum W_i X_i)^2}$$

Where $W_i = \frac{1}{\sigma_i^2}$.

HK causes t tests to become invalid. Monte Carlo experiments show that when OLS is infected by HK and takes into account HK, OLS variances are biased upwards, OLS standard errors are biased upwards and thus OLS t stats are biased downwards. So under OLS, there is an increased chance of making a type 2 error, $\hat{\beta}$ may be wrongly concluded to be insignificant when it is actually significant under the BLUE WLS.

---

[10] Note that WLS is a subset of Generalized Least Squares (GLS).

OLS and WLS Confidence Intervals

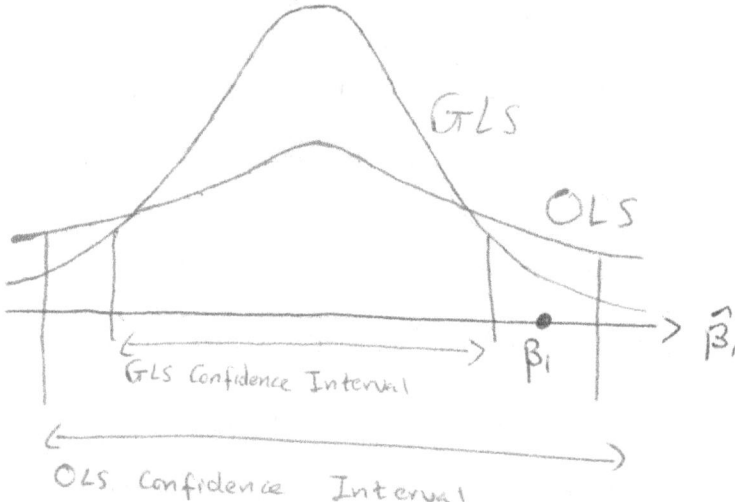

Additionally, because OLS variances are upward biased, RSS is upwards biased, ESS is downward biased, the F stat falsely becomes more statistically insignificant and so our joint inferential statements are invalid.

Worse yet, if we disregard HK altogether and do not incorporate HK into OLS then we do not even know if our OLS variances are under-estimated or over-estimated and our inferential statements become even more invalid /confusing.

Detection
Many different methods/tests can be used to detect HK including:

Graphical Method
Simply plot $\hat{u}_i^2$ against the regressors and check for patterns. If a pattern emerges then HK may be present.

Possible HK Patterns

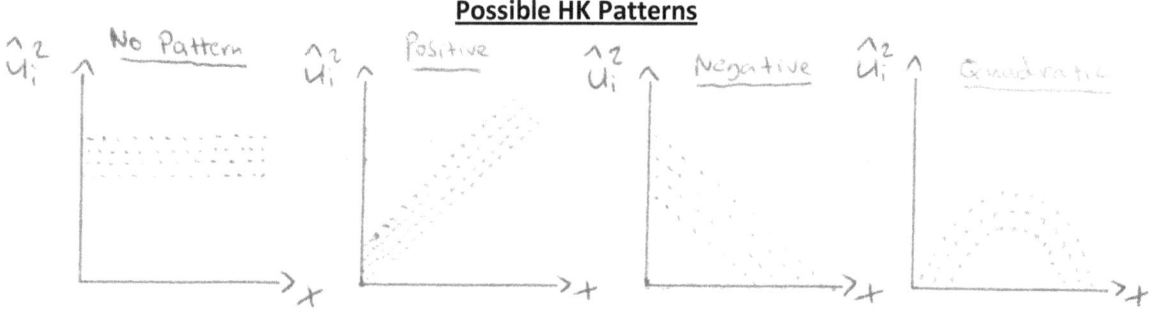

Park Test
Park formalizes the graphical method. Park suggests that HK may take the form $Var(u_i) = f(X_i)$ and proposes the following functional forms:

$$\sigma_i^2 = \sigma^2 X_i^\beta e^{v_i}$$

Or:

$$ln\sigma_i^2 = ln\sigma^2 + \beta ln X_i + V_i$$

Note that σ_i^2 may be unknown so we must use $\hat{u}_i^2$ as a proxy.

The Park test has the following steps:

1) Regress one of the models above.

2) $H_0: No\ HK\ \beta = 0$

   $H_1: HK\ \beta \neq 0$

3) t test β and if β is significant at the chosen level of significance then reject the null hypothesis, HK is present because $\hat{u}_i^2$ moves with X_i.

But:
- The error term V_i may suffer HK, so the Park test is only an exploratory test.

Goldfeld-Quandt Test
Assumption: HK variance σ_i^2 is positively related to a regressor. Maybe we have:

$$\sigma_i^2 = \sigma^2 X_i^2$$

As the regressor increases in value, so does σ_i^2.

Goldfeld-Quandt has the following steps:

1) Rank X_i in ascending order.

2) c = 2n/8 or specified a priori. Omit c middle observations. You are left with two groups of X_i values, the highest and lowest.

3) 1st group of lower X_i values are the smaller variance group, obtain RSS_1.

   2nd group of higher X_i values are the higher variance group, obtain RSS_2.

4) $H_o: No\ HK$, equal variance in both groups.

   $H_1: HK$, unequal variance between the two groups.

5) $F\ stat = \frac{RSS_2/df}{RSS_1/df} \sim F(df, df)$

   Where df = ((n-c)/2) – k.

6) If the F stat > the F critical value at the chosen level of significance then reject the null hypothesis, HK is present.

But:
- Must omit c observations to accentuate differences in the variance between the two groups. By doing this we lose degrees of freedom so the power of the test falls.
- We must know what regressor is proportional to σ_i^2.
- We must assume u_i are normally distributed.

Breusch-Pagan-Godfrey (BPG) Test

Assumption: σ_i^2 is a linear function of all/some of the regressors:

$$\sigma_i^2 = \alpha_1 + \alpha_2 Z_{2i} + \alpha_3 Z_{3i} + \cdots + \alpha_m Z_{mi}$$

Where Z_{mi} are the regressors suspected of being related to σ_i^2.

The Breusch-Godfrey-Pagan (BPG) test has the following steps:

1) Regress the original model:

$$y_i = \beta_1 + \beta_2 X_{2i} + \beta_3 X_{3i} + \cdots + \beta_k X_{ki} + u_i$$

Obtain $\hat{u}_i$.

2) $\hat{\sigma}^2 = \frac{\sum \hat{u}_i^2}{n}$.

3) $p_i = \frac{\hat{u}_i^2}{\hat{\sigma}^2}$.

4) Regress p_i on Zs:

$$p_i = \alpha_1 + \alpha_2 Z_{2i} + \alpha_3 Z_{3i} + \cdots + \alpha_m Z_{mi} + v_i$$

And obtain ESS_p.

5) H_o: No HK.

   H_1: HK.

6) $\theta = \frac{ESS_p}{2} \sim X^2_{m-1}$.

7) If the θ stat > the chi-square critical value at the chosen level of significance then reject the null hypothesis, HK is present.

Advantages:
- A general and flexible test.
- A powerful test in large samples.
- Does not need to know which regressor is related to σ_i^2.

But:
- Assumes u_i are normally distributed. The BPG test is sensitive to small departures from normality.
- Only detects linear forms of HK.
- White's general HK test could discover HK when the BPG test does not.

White's General HK Test
A relatively simple test that can detect both pure HK and HK caused by model misspecification.

White's general HK test has the following steps:

1) Regress the original model:

$$y_i = \beta_1 + \beta_2 X_{2i} + \beta_3 X_{3i} + u_i$$

And obtain $\hat{u}_i$.

2) Run the auxiliary regression:

$$\hat{u}_i^2 = \alpha_1 + \alpha_2 X_{2i} + \alpha_3 X_{3i} + \alpha_4 X_{2i}^2 + \alpha_5 X_{3i}^2 + \alpha_6 X_2 X_3 + v_i$$

And obtain R_A^2.

3) $H_0: No\ HK, \alpha_2 = \alpha_3 = \cdots = \alpha_k = 0$.

    $H_1: HK$, at least one $\alpha_k \neq 0$.

4) $n.R_A^2 \sim X_{k-1}^2$

    Where n is the sample size and k-1 is the degrees of freedom in the auxiliary regression.

5) If the $n.R_A^2$ stat > the chi-square critical value at the chosen level of significance then reject the null hypothesis, HK is present.

Advantages:
- Detects pure HK if there is no cross product term ($\alpha_6 X_2 X_3$) in the auxiliary regression. Detects pure HK or HK caused by model misspecification if the cross product term is included in the auxiliary regression.
- Do not need prior knowledge of the nature of HK.
- Linear and nonlinear forms of HK can be detected.
- Do not need normality assumption.

But:
- Does not reveal which factors or variables are driving HK.
- Many regressors in the auxiliary regression decrease degrees of freedom. Although, White's general HK test can be modified with $\hat{y}_i$ and $\hat{y}_i^2$ substituted in for the Xs to preserve degrees of freedom.

Koenker-Basset HK Test
A simple test, the Koenker-Basset HK test has the following steps:

1) Regress the original model:

$$y_i = \beta_1 + \beta_2 X_{2i} + \beta_3 X_{3i} + \cdots + \beta_k X_{ki} + u_i$$

And obtain $\hat{u}_i$.

2) Regress:

$$\hat{u}_i^2 = \alpha_1 + \alpha_2 \hat{y}_i^2 + v_i$$

3) $H_o: No\ HK, \alpha_2 = 0$

   $H_1: HK, \alpha_2 \neq 0$

4) t test α_2. If α_2 is significant at the chosen level of significance then reject the null hypothesis, HK is present.

Advantages:
- Does not need normality assumption.

Remedies

Many remedies could be used to cure HK including:

Weighted Least Squares (WLS)

Weighted Least Squares (WLS) is the BLUE estimator when HK is present. WLS is Generalized Least Squares (GLS) but with weights to minimize $RSS = \frac{\hat{u}_i^2}{\sigma_i^2}$. By weighting observations with weights $\frac{1}{\sigma_i}$ WLS gives more weigh to observations that have a lower variance (and are therefore more accurate) and gives less weight to observations that have a higher variance (and are therefore inaccurate).

Let's say we have the model:

$$y_i = \beta_1 + \beta_2 X_{2i} + u_i$$

And there is HK because:

$$E(u_i^2) = \sigma_i^2$$

As long as we know σ_i^2 we can weight the HK plagued model with weights $W_i = \frac{1}{\sigma_i}$:

$$\left(\frac{y_i}{\sigma_i}\right) = \beta_1 \left(\frac{X_{oi}}{\sigma_i}\right) + \beta_2 \left(\frac{X_{2i}}{\sigma_i}\right) + \left(\frac{u_i}{\sigma_i}\right)$$

Where X_{oi} is equal to 1.

And the new variance of the error term is:

$$Var\left(\frac{u_i}{\sigma_i}\right) = E\left(\frac{u_i}{\sigma_i}\right)^2 = \frac{1}{\sigma_i^2} E(u_i^2) = \frac{\sigma_i^2}{\sigma_i^2} = 1$$

So $Var\left(\frac{u_i}{\sigma_i}\right) = 1$, the new WLS variance of the error term is constant and not plagued by HK. OLS on this WLS transformed regression model will be BLUE.

But:
- We must know the weights $W_i = \frac{1}{\sigma_i}$. Otherwise we must use White's robust standard errors.
- HK tests may still indicate HK after WLS has been applied, if this happens then the WLS transformation may be wrong and different weights must be tried.

Robust Standard Errors
White's HK robust standard errors allow asymptotically valid statistical inferences to be made when HK is present.

Let's say we cannot make valid inferential statements because our model is plagued by HK, our variances are wrong:

$$Var(\beta_2) = \frac{\sum X_i^2 \sigma_i^2}{(\sum X_i^2)^2}$$

We do not know σ_i^2 but we can use $\hat{u}_i^2$ as a proxy:

$$Robust\ Var(\beta_2) = \frac{\sum X_i^2 \hat{u}_i^2}{(\sum X_i^2)^2}$$

$$Robust\ s.e.(\beta_2) = \sqrt{\frac{\sum X_i^2 \hat{u}_i^2}{(\sum X_i^2)^2}}$$

Advantages:
- Simple and easy to use, should always be given with regression models.
- Do not need to know σ_i^2.

Model Correction
Maybe the correct model has a homoskedastic variance and the only problem is a misspecified model causing HK. The solution is simply to correct the functional form or add the omitted regressors(s) to make $Var(u_i)$ homoskedastic.

Log
A log transformation could decrease the extent of HK. A log transformation compresses the scales in which the variables are measured and can reduce a tenfold difference between two values to a two fold difference.

But:
- logs cannot be applied to negative values.

Do Nothing
OLS could still be BLUE when HK is present but this is extremely rare. The Gauss-Markov conditions are necessary but not sufficient for OLS to be BLUE. The necessary and sufficient conditions for OLS to be BLUE is given by Kruskal's theorem.

Autocorrelation

Autocorrelation (AC) Detection

Autocorrelation (AC)[11] is correlation between the error term ordered in time or space. AC makes the error term follow a distinct pattern. Basically, u_t depends on u_{t-1}. $Cov(u_t, u_{t-1}) \neq 0$. AC means $\sigma_{ij} \neq 0$ for $i \neq j$.

AC could follow any of the patterns shown below:

AC Patterns

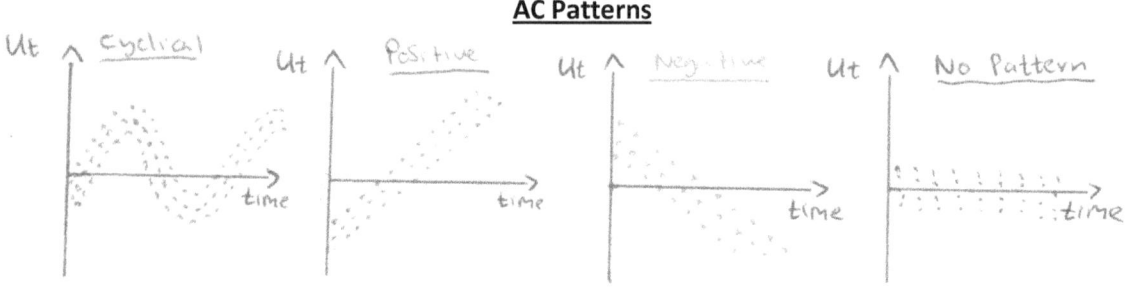

Causalities

AC may be caused by numerous factors including:

1) Nonstationarity. A time series is nonstationary if its mean/variance/covariance vary over time. If X and/or Y are nonstationary then u_t may be nonstationary too.

2) Lags. If a statistically significant lag is not included in a model then u_t will soak up its explanatory power and follow a systematic pattern.

3) Model misspecification. Omitted variables bias means u_t soaks up the explanatory power of the missing variable and then follows a pattern. Moreover, the wrong functional form, for example, using a linear instead of a quadratic functional form, can cause u_t to follow a pattern.

4) Manipulation of data. Manipulating raw data, for example, by turning data into averages, dampens fluctuations which can then be soaked up by u_t and make u_t follow a pattern.

5) Inertia. Business cycles move cyclically with self-sustaining upswings and downswings so u_t depends on u_{t-1}.

Consequences

AC infects the variances of OLS estimates and causes inferential statements to become invalid, OLS is no longer BLUE.

Let's say u_t follows an AR(1) scheme:

$$u_t = pu_{t-1} + \varepsilon_t$$

Where ε_t is white noise.

---

[11] See Appendix A for the matrix notation of AC consequences.

Let's look at the OLS variance of $\hat{\beta}$:

$$Var(\hat{\beta}_1)_{OLS} = \frac{\sigma^2}{(\sum x_t^2)}$$

And the AR(1) variance of $\hat{\beta}$, that is, the OLS variance of $\hat{\beta}$ when AC is accounted for:

$$Var(\hat{\beta}_1)_{AR1} = \frac{\sigma^2}{(\sum x_t^2)}\left[1 + 2p\frac{\sum x_t x_{t-1}}{\sum x_t^2} + \cdots + 2p^{n-1}\frac{\sum x_1 x_n}{\sum x_t^2}\right]$$

AC causes t tests to become invalid. Assuming there is positive AC and this is unaccounted for by OLS, then OLS variances are biased downwards, OLS standard errors are biased downwards and thus OLS t stats are biased upwards. So under OLS, there is an increased chance of making a type 1 error, $\hat{\beta}$ may be wrongly concluded to be significant when it is actually insignificant under the AR(1) variance.

OLS and AR(1) Confidence Intervals

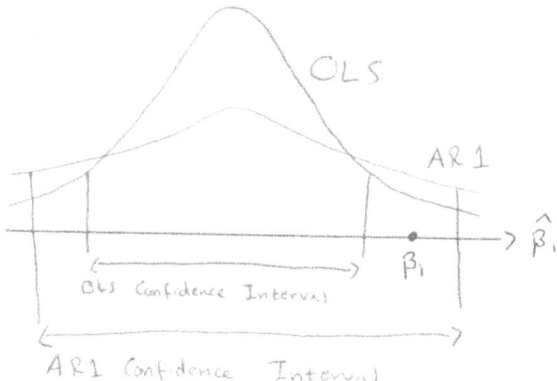

Additionally, because OLS variances are downward biased, RSS is downwards biased, ESS is upward biased, the F stat falsely becomes more statistically significant and so our joint inferential statements are invalid.

Detection
Many different methods/tests can be used to detect AC including:

Graphical Method
Simply plot $\hat{u}_t$ against $\hat{u}_{t-1}$ and check for patterns. If a pattern emerges then AC may be present.

Durbin-Watson d-Test
Assumptions:
- The regression model includes an intercept term. If it does not include an intercept term then use the dL minimum bound.
- Regressors are nonstochastic.
- Disturbances are generated by an AR(1) scheme only.
- The error term is normally distributed.
- The regression model is not autoregressive, that is, it does not include lagged regressands as regressors. Otherwise the d stat is biased towards 2.
- No missing observations in the data.

The d stat:

$$d = \frac{\sum_{t=2}^{t=n}(\hat{u}_t - \hat{u}_{t-1})^2}{\sum_{t=1}^{t=n}\hat{u}_t^2} = \frac{\sum \hat{u}_t^2 + \sum \hat{u}_{t-1}^2 + 2\sum \hat{u}_t \hat{u}_{t-1}}{\sum \hat{u}_t^2}$$

And since $\sum \hat{u}_t \approx \sum \hat{u}_{t-1}$ then:

$$d \approx 2\left(1 - \frac{\sum \hat{u}_t \hat{u}_{t-1}}{\sum \hat{u}_t^2}\right)$$

And because $\frac{\sum \hat{u}_t \hat{u}_{t-1}}{\sum \hat{u}_t^2} = \hat{p}$:

$$d \approx 2(1 - \hat{p})$$

The null hypothesis is H_o: No AC.
And the alternative hypothesis is H_1: AC.

Next we must find the d critical values, the d upper bound (dU) and the d lower bound (dL) from the Durbin-Watson d table for n and (k-1) degrees of freedom and set up the decision zones:

Durbin-Watson Decision Zones

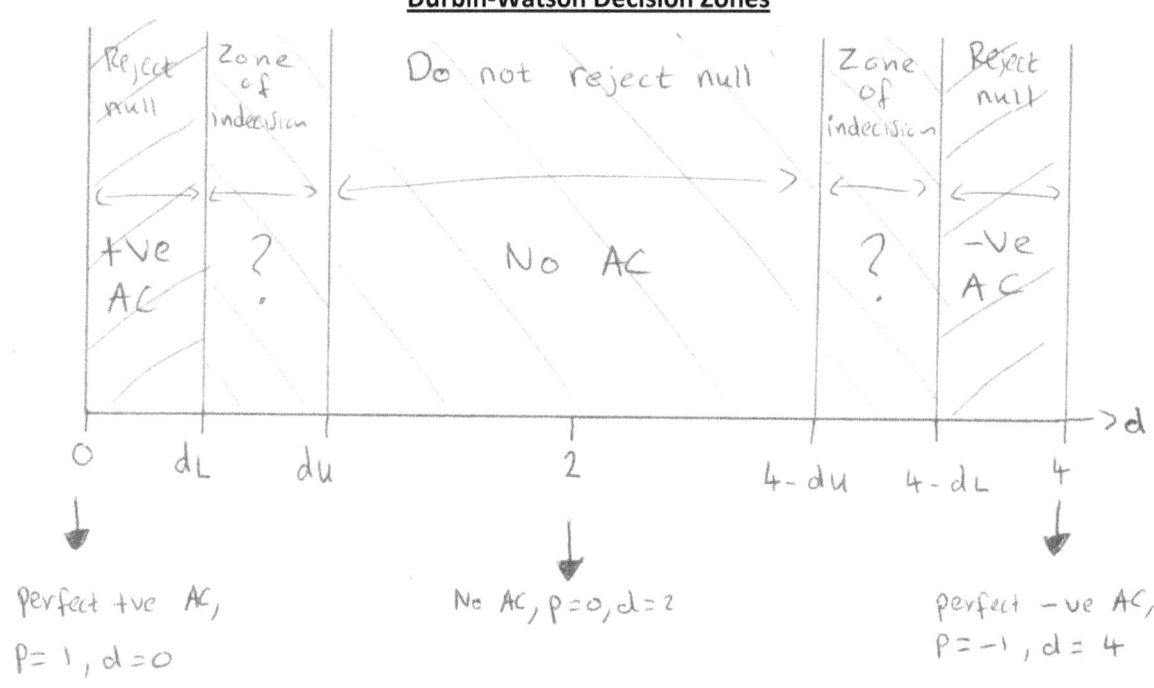

If the d stat falls within the far left or far right areas then reject the null hypothesis of no AC, AC is present (positive AC in the far left area and negative AC in the far right area). If the d stat falls in the middle area then do not reject the null hypothesis, AC is not present. If the d stat falls in either of the zones of indecision then we cannot make a decision on the presence of AC.

Advantages:
- A good small sample test. But note that as the sample size falls too low, the d lower bound falls and the d upper bound rises and the zone of indecision widens.
- Reasoably robust to heteroskedasticity and non-normality.
- Both AR(1) and moving average AC structures can be detected.

But:
- The d test needs the assumptions to hold, for example, normality.
- The d test does not detect AR(2) AC.
- The d test cannot test an autoregressive model.
- If the d stat falls in the zone of indecision then we cannot really decide on the presence of AC.

Bresuch-Godfrey LM Test

AC can be detected by the Breusch-Godfrey (BG) test for any AR(p) process with/without lagged dependent variables as regressors. Note that the p in AR(p) for the BG test can be determined by the frequency of the variables.

The BG test has the following steps:

1) Regress the original model:

$$y_t = \beta_1 + \beta_2 X_{2t} + u_t$$

And obtain $\hat{u}_t$.

2) Run an auxiliary regression of $\hat{u}_t$ on all the regressors and on all the lagged values of $\hat{u}_t$:

$$\hat{u}_t = \alpha_1 + \alpha_2 X_{2t} + \hat{p}_1 \hat{u}_{t-1} + \cdots + \hat{p}_p \hat{u}_{t-p} + \varepsilon_t$$

And obtain R^2.

3) $H_o: p_1 = p_2 = \cdots = p_p = 0$, no AC of any order.

$H_1: At\ least\ one\ p_p \neq 0$, AC of some order.

4) The LM test statistic $n.R^2 \sim X_p^2$.

5) If $n.R^2$ is greater than the chi-square critical value for the chosen level of significance then reject the null hypothesis, some order of AC is present. If $n.R^2$ is less than the chi-square critical value for the chosen level of significance then do not reject the null, AC is not present.

Advantages:
- A good all-round general test.
- Allows for nonstochastic regressors and an autoregressive model.
- Allows for higher order AR(p) schemes.
- Allows for any order moving average of the white noise error term in the AR(p) scheme.
- A good large sample test.

But:
- Low power in small samples (frequently fails to reject a false null hypothesis).
- The lag structure cannot be specified a priori, it needs to be toyed with. Although, we can use the Akaike Information Criteria to select the lag length.
- Assumes $\hat{u}_t$ in step 2 is homoskedastic.

Remedies
Many remedies could be used to cure AC including:

Generalized Least Squares (GLS)
Apply the Generalized Least Squares (GLS) quasi-difference transformation to cure a model infected by AC.

Let's say the original AC plagued regression model is:

$$y_t = \beta_1 + \beta_2 X_t + u_t$$

And, for simplicity, assume the error term follows an AR(1) scheme:

$$u_t = p u_{t-1} + \varepsilon_t$$

Lagging the original model by 1 period and multiplying it by p gives:

$$p y_{t-1} = p\beta_1 + p\beta_2 X_{t-1} + p u_{t-1}$$

Minus this from the original model to get:

$$y_t - p y_{t-1} = \beta_1(1-p) + \beta_2(X_t - p X_{t-1}) + (u_t - p u_{t-1})$$

And thus the GLS quasi-differenced model is:

$$y_t^* = \beta_1^* + \beta_2^* X_t^* + \varepsilon_t$$

AC is gone now because the error term in the quasi-differenced model ε_t is the white noise error term from the AR(1) scheme. ε_t follows the CLRM assumptions $E(\varepsilon_t) = 0$, $Var(\varepsilon_t) = \sigma_\varepsilon^2$ and $Cov(\varepsilon_t, \varepsilon_{t+s}) = 0 \; for \; s \neq 0$ so there is no more AC.

But:
- By quasi-differencing we lose 1 degree of freedom because the 1st observation has no antecedent. This could be particularly problematic if our sample size is small. The solution is to use the Prais-Winston transformation for the first y_t^* and X_t^*:

$$y_t^* = y_t \sqrt{1-p^2}$$

$$X_t^* = X_t \sqrt{1-p^2}$$

Now our estimates perfectly mimic Generalized Least Squares and are BLUE.
- Note that we must know p. If we do not know p then we must estimate it.

Estimated Generalized Least Squares (EGLS)
If we must estimate p then we are using Estimated Generalized Least Squares (EGLS). Many methods are available to estimate p including:

Rearranging the d Stat

$$\hat{p} \approx 1 - \frac{d}{2}$$

Rearranging the AR(1) Scheme

$$\hat{p} = \frac{\hat{u}_t - \varepsilon_t}{\hat{u}_{t-1}}$$

Rearranging the Prais-Winston Transformation

$$\hat{p} = \sqrt{1 - \left(\frac{y_t^*}{y_t}\right)^2}$$

Cochrane-Orcutt Iterative Method

The Cochrane-Orcutt iterative method begins with the following three equations:

(A) $y_t = \beta_1 + \beta_2 X_t + u_t$

(B) $u_t = p u_{t-1} + \varepsilon_t$

(C) $y_t - p y_{t-1} = \beta_1(1-p) + \beta_2(X_t - pX_{t-1}) + \varepsilon_t$

And then we either use the 2 step method or the iterative method:

---

2 Step Method

1 - Regress (A) and obtain $\hat{u}_t$.

2 - Regress $\hat{u}_t = p\hat{u}_{t-1} + e_t$ and obtain $\hat{p}$.

3 - Substitute $\hat{p}$ into (C) to get $y_t - \hat{p} y_{t-1} = \beta_1(1-\hat{p}) + \beta_2(X_t - \hat{p}X_{t-1}) + v_t$ and create new variables:
$y_t^* = \beta_1^* + \beta_2^* X_t^* + v_t$. $\hat{\beta}_1 = \frac{\beta_1^*}{(1-\hat{p})}$ and $\hat{\beta}_2 = \hat{\beta}_2^*$.

Iterative Method

4 - Substitute in $\hat{\beta}_1$ and $\hat{\beta}_2$ into (A) and get $\hat{u}_t^*$.

5 - Regress $\hat{u}_t^* = p^* \hat{u}_{t-1}^* + e_t$ and obtain $\hat{p}^*$.

6 - Substitute $\hat{p}^*$ into (C) to get $y_t - \hat{p}^* y_{t-1} = \beta_1(1-\hat{p}^*) + \beta_2(X_t - \hat{p}^*X_{t-1}) + v_t$ and create new variables:
$y_t^{**} = \beta_1^{**} + \beta_2^{**} X_t^{**} + v_t$. $\hat{\beta}_1 = \frac{\beta_1^{**}}{(1-\hat{p}^*)}$ and $\hat{\beta}_2 = \hat{\beta}_2^{**}$.

7 - Repeat the process until $\hat{p}$ from 2 successive iterations changes by a specified value (for example, 0.0001).

Fully Estimated Generalized Least Squares (FEGLS)
Fully Estimated Generalized Least Squares (FEGLS) is EGLS but with the Prais-Winston transformation for the first observations in the quasi-difference regression.

Model Correction
If AC is caused by model misspecification then just correct the functional form or add any omitted regressors.

Newey-West Standard Errors
We could continue to use OLS but correct the s.e.($\hat{\beta}$) by using Newey-West standard errors.

Let's say we have the model:

$$y_t = \beta_1 + \beta_2 X_{2t} + \cdots + \beta_k X_{kt} + u_t$$

Run the auxiliary regression:

$$X_{2t} = \delta_1 + \delta_2 X_{3t} + \cdots + \delta_k X_{(k+1)t} + r_t$$

And the variance of the auxiliary regression is:

$$AxVar(\hat{\beta}_2) = \left(\sum E(r_t^2)\right)^2 Var\left(\sum r_t u_t\right)$$

Making the robust standard error:

$$s.e.(\hat{\beta}_2)^{Newey} = \left(\frac{s.e.(\beta_2)}{\hat{\sigma}}\right)^2 \sqrt{AxVar(\hat{\beta}_2)}$$

$s.e.(\hat{\beta}_2)^{Newey}$ is robust to both AC and heteroskedasticity.

But:
- It assumes an asymptotically large sample.

Do Nothing
OLS could still be BLUE when AC is present but this is extremely rare. The Gauss-Markov conditions are necessary but not sufficient for OLS to be BLUE. The necessary and sufficient conditions for OLS to be BLUE is given by Kruskal's theorem.

Koyck Transformation

Start with an infinite distributed lag model (IDL):

$$y_t = \alpha + \partial_o Z_t + \partial_1 Z_{t-1} + \partial_2 Z_{t-2} + \cdots + u_t$$

This relates y_t to all past Z_t through an infinite past. As $j \to \infty$, $\partial_j \to 0$.

But, we cannot estimate an infinite amount of lags with only a finite amount of data, we cannot estimate the infinite number of parameters. There may be a multicollinearity problem too because there is an infinite amount of regressors. Instead, we can use the Koyck transformation to turn the IDL model into an estimate-able model. The Koyck transformation makes the model simpler to estimate whilst still including an infinite number of lags.

Assuming the ∂_j are all the same sign and that they decline geometrically:

$$\partial_j = \gamma p^j$$

Where $|p| < 1$ for j = 0, 1, 2, …

And as $j \to \infty$, $\partial_j \to 0$, just as in the IDL mode.

The impact multiplier is:

$$\partial_0 = \gamma p^o = \gamma$$

And since:

$$1 + p + p^2 + \cdots + p^j = \frac{1}{(1-p)}$$

the long-run multiplier is:

$$\frac{\gamma}{(1-p)}$$

Then sub γp^j into the IDL and assume the IDL holds in periods t and t-1 to get:

(A) $y_t = \alpha + \gamma Z_t + \gamma p Z_{t-1} + \gamma p^2 Z_{t-2} + \cdots + u_t$

(B) $y_{t-1} = \alpha + \gamma Z_{t-1} + \gamma p Z_{t-2} + \gamma p^2 Z_{t-3} + \cdots + u_{t-1}$

Multiply (B) by p and minus it from (A) to get:

$$y_t - p y_{t-1} = (1-p)\alpha + \gamma Z_t + u_t - u_{t-1}$$

$$y_t = (1-p)\alpha + \gamma Z_t + p y_{t-1} + u_t - u_{t-1}$$

Now we can estimate γ, p and α.

But:
- The model becomes an autoregressive model since y_{t-1} is on the right-hand side. This may be problematic because an endogeneity problem could occur, y_{t-1} may be correlated with u_{t-1} and this causes a heterogeneity bias and inconsistency. The solution is then to use an instrumental variable for y_{t-1}.
- There may be autocorrelation. But, u_t may follow an AR(1) scheme:

$$u_t = pu_{t-1} + \varepsilon_t$$

So:

$$u_t - pu_{t-1} = \varepsilon_t$$

So ε_t in the Koyck model is just white noise and there is no autocorrelation in this situation.
- The Koyck transformation is an algebraic process devoid of theoretical underpinnings. Maybe you should use the Adaptive Expectations model should be used instead. The Stock Adjustment model is another alternative and also a rationalisation of the Koyck transformation, that is, it comes to predict the same model as Koyck but through economic theory.

Spurious Regression

Assume Y_t and X_t are both I(1) and independent. Because Y_t and X_t are both I(1), their linear combination and residuals are also I(1). So regressing X_t on Y_t could lead to a spurious regression (or nonsense regression), that is, a high R^2 and significant t and F stats even though there is no meaningful theoretical relationship between them. Running the regression:

$$Y_t = \beta_0 + \beta_1 X_t + U_t$$

Y_t and X_t should have no relationship but if there is spurious regression then β_1 is non-zero and statistically significant. Regression analysis suggests a relationship exists between the variables when no causal relationship exists. Both t and F tests are biased towards rejecting the correct null hypothesis of no relationship and accepting a spurious relationship. Moreover, as the sample size increases, it becomes more likely that the null hypothesis $H_0: \beta_2 = 0$ will be wrongly rejected.

Note that Granger's rule of thumb suggests there is spurious regression if:

$$R^2 > d$$

Where d is the Durbin-Watson d statistic.

The solution is to difference Y_t and X_t. Above, we would first-difference the regression equation to get ΔY_t and ΔX_t and then regress ΔX_t on ΔY_t to get:

$$\Delta Y_t = \beta_0 + \beta_1 \Delta X_t + U_t$$

Now β_1 should be very close to zero and statistically insignificant.

Time Stationarity

Stationary
A time series x_t is stationary if its probability distribution is stable over time (time invariant), that is, if x_t has a mean $E(x_t)$ and variance $E(x_t^2)$ that does not change overtime and its covariance $cov(x_t, x_{t-h})$ between any two time periods depends only on h and not t.

Assume an AR(1) process:

$$x_t = \rho x_{t-1} + e_t$$

Where e_t is white noise error IID $(0, \sigma_e^2)$ and t = 1, ..., T.

This AR(1) process is stationary if ρ < 1 because:

A) $E(x_t) = \rho E(x_{t-1}) + E(e_t) = \rho E(x_{t-1}) = \rho E(x_t)$, the mean is time invariant.

B) $E(x_t^2) = \rho^2 E(x_{t-1}^2) + E(e_t^2)$, so, $\sigma_x^2 = \rho^2 \sigma_x^2 + \sigma_e^2 = \frac{\sigma_e^2}{(1-\rho^2)}$, the variance is time invariant.

C) $Cov(x_t, x_{t-h}) = Cov(\rho x_{t-1}^2 + x_{t-h} e_t) = \rho E(x_t^2) = \rho \sigma_x^2$, the covariance is time invariant.

White Noise
White noise is a purely random process. Let's say we have:

$$x_t = e_t$$

Where e_t is IID $(0, \sigma_e^2)$ and t = 1, ..., T.

White noise error, x_t has the following properties:

A) A zero and constant mean $E(e_t) = 0$ for all t.

B) Constant variance $Var(x_t) = Var(e_t) = \sigma^2$ for all t.

C) Constant covariance $Cov(x_t, x_{t-k}) = 0$.

So the white noise process is stationary because all of its moments are time invariant.

Nonstationary
A random variable x_t is nonstationary if it has a unit root, that is, if p=1 in the AR(1) process. This could result in either a random walk or a random walk with drift.

Random Walk
A random walk is an AR(1) scheme with a unit root, that is, p = 1:

$$x_t = x_{t-1} + \varepsilon_t$$

Where ε_t is a random shock and is IID $(0, \sigma_\varepsilon^2)$ and t = 1, ..., T.

A random walk has an infinite memory and remembers the random shocks ε_t forever. The ε_t have a permanent effect on x_t but sum up to zero.

A random walk is nonstationary because:

A) It has a zero and constant mean $E(x_t) = \rho E(x_{t-1}) + E(\Sigma e_t) = E(x_{t-1}) = E(x_t)$ so the mean is time invariant.

B) It has a time variant variance $E(y_t^2) = E(e_t) + E(e_{t-1}) + \cdots + E(e_1) = \sigma_e^2 t$ so this moment is nonstationary.

C) It has a time variant correlation coefficient $Corr(x_t, x_{t+h}) = \sqrt{\frac{t}{t+h}}$ so the correlation coefficient is nonstationary.

Random Walk with Drift
A random walk with drift is an AR(1) scheme with a unit root p = 1 and a drift parameter a_o:

$$x_t = a_o + x_{t-1} + \varepsilon_t$$

Where ε_t is a random shock and is IID (0, σ_ε^2) and t = 1, …, T.

A random walk with drift has an infinite memory and remembers the random shocks ε_t forever. The ε_t have a permanent effect on x_t but sum up to zero.

A random walk with drift is nonstationary because:

A) It has a time variant mean $E(x_t) = t. E(a_o) + E(x_o) + E(\varepsilon_1) + E(\varepsilon_2) + \cdots + E(\varepsilon_t) = t. a_o + x_o$ so the mean is nonstationary.

B) It has a time variant variance $Var(x_t) = Var(t. a_0 + x_o + \varepsilon_1 + \varepsilon_2 + \cdots + \varepsilon_t) = t. Var(a_0) + Var(x_o) + Var(\varepsilon_1) + Var(\varepsilon_2) + \cdots + Var(\varepsilon_t) = 0 + 0 + \sigma^2 + \sigma^2 + \cdots + \sigma^2 = t. \sigma^2$ so the variance is nonstationary.

Making a Time Series Stationary
A nonstationary time series can become stationary if it is first-differenced. Let's say we have a random walk:

$$x_t = x_{t-1} + \varepsilon_t$$

Where ε_t is a random shock and is IID (0, σ_ε^2) and t = 1, …, T.

First-difference x_t by subtracting x_{t-1} from both sides:

$$x_t - x_{t-1} = x_{t-1} - x_{t-1} + e_t$$

$$\Delta x_t = e_t$$

The first-difference Δx_t is weakly dependent because it is white noise and IID (0, σ_e^2). By first-differencing, we effectively rob and appropriate the time stationary properties of the white noise error term in the AR(1) process. Δx_t has a time stationary mean $E(\Delta x_t) = E(e_t) = 0$ and variance $var(\Delta x_t) = var(e_t) = \sigma_e^2$.

A variable x_t, is integrated of order one I(1) if its level term x_t is nonstationary and its first-difference Δx_t is stationary. A variable is I(d) integrated of order d if it must be differenced d times to make it stationary.

Unit Root Tests

A unit root may be detected by using either the Dickey-Fuller test, Augmented Dickey-Fuller test, Phillips-Perron test and/or the KPSS test.

Dickey-Fuller Test
A test to detect whether a time series has a unit root and is I(1) is the Dickey-Fuller (DF) test. Let's say x_t follows a simple AR(1) process:

$$x_t = \rho x_{t-1} + e_t$$

For convenience subtract x_{t-1} from both sides:

$$x_t - x_{t-1} = \rho x_{t-1} - x_{t-1} + e_t$$

$$\Delta x_t = \theta x_{t-1} + e_t$$

where θ = ρ - 1

x_t has a unit root and is I(1) when ρ = 1 or conversely when θ = 0. And x_t is weakly dependent and I(0) when ρ < 1 or conversely θ < 0.

The DF test has the following steps:

1) Regress:

$$\Delta x_t = \theta x_{t-1} + e_t$$

2) Obtain the t statistic $t_{\hat{\theta}}$ for the estimated coefficient $\hat{\theta}$.

3) Set up the null hypothesis H_0: θ = 0 and ρ = 1, x_t is I(1). And the one-sided alternative hypothesis H_1: θ < 0 and ρ < 1, x_t is I(0).

4) Obtain the DF critical value c for the chosen level of significance.

5) And finally, compare $t_{\hat{\theta}}$ with c. Assuming $t_{\hat{\theta}}$ and c are both negative, if $|t_{\hat{\theta}}| > |c|$ then reject H_0, x_t is I(0). If $|t_{\hat{\theta}}| < |c|$ then do not reject H_0, x_t is I(1).

Firstly, note that H_1: θ < 0 and ρ < 1 is a one-sided alternative. We do not consider a two-sided alternative as it is very rare that ρ > 1 because this is explosive. Secondly, under H_0: θ = 0 and ρ = 1, x_t is nonstationary and I(1) so the Central Limit Theorem used to justify the asymptotic normal distribution for the t statistic does not hold. The asymptotic distribution of $t_{\hat{\theta}}$ under H_0 is instead the DF distribution. So we must use the DF critical values for our t tests.

A cautionary note must be made about the residuals used in the DF test. The residuals in the AR(1) process $\Delta x_t = \theta x_{t-1} + e_t$ could be plagued by autocorrelation (AC) and/or heteroskedasticity (HK). AC and HK infect OLS standard errors and thus cause the DF test's inferential statements to become invalid.

Augmented Dickey-Fuller Test

AC in the DF test could be due to a dynamically incomplete specification of the AR(1) process and, in this situation, requires adding lags of Δx_t as regressors. After enough lags of Δx_t are added AC should disappear. When the DF test incorporates lags of Δx_t in this manner it becomes the Augmented Dickey-Fuller (ADF) test. Basically, the ADF test follows the same steps as those in the DF test outlined before but step 1 starts with the following regression:

$$\Delta x_t = \theta x_{t-1} + \Delta x_{t-1} + \Delta x_{t-2} + \Delta x_{t-m} + e_t$$

Note that:
- The Schwarze-Bazian Information Criteria (SBC) or the Akaike Information Criteria (AIC) can be used to select the lag length (m) of Δx_t.
- Should a time trend be included? It is crucial not to omit a necessary time trend otherwise ADF inferential statements are invalid. Likewise, omitting an unnecessary time trend makes the ADF test more powerful. It is best to start with a time trend and use a t test to test its significance (using the DF critical values rather than the t critical values) and if the time trend is insignificant then remove it.

Augmented Dickey-Fuller Test or Phillips-Perron Test?

If AC is found but HK is not found then the ADF test should be used. If either AC is not found and HK is found, or both AC and HK are found, then the Phillips-Perron (PP) test should instead be used to test if x_t is I(1) because the PP test is more powerful than the ADF test under these circumstances. The PP test basically mirrors the ADF test but adjusts the standard errors used to calculate the t stat by using Newey-West standard errors to remedy the HK and/or AC infection.

KPSS Test

Another unit root and I(1) test is the KPSS test. Although, unlike the ADF and PP tests, the KPSS test tests the null hypothesis of I(0) against the alternative of I(1). The KPSS test calculates an LM stat and uses a 5% critical value c of 0.146 and 0.463 for a trended and non-trended series respectively. If $|LM| > |c|$ reject Ho, the series is I(1). If $|LM| < |c|$ do not reject Ho, the series is I(0).

Cointegration

A pair of 2 I(1) variables are cointegrated if their linear combination:

$$y_t - \beta_1 - \beta_2 x_t = Z_t$$

is white noise, I(0) and therefore stationary.

Although both y_t and x_t may have stochastic trends, they are cointegrated because they are kept together by a long-run equilibrium relationship. Any deviations from equilibrium will be in the short-run only because the cointegrating parameter β_2 pulls them back together.

Cointegration

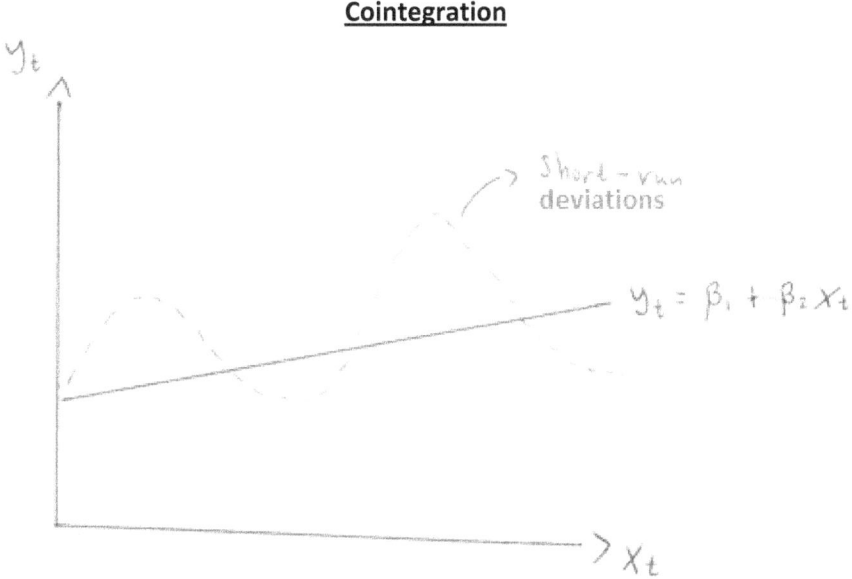

Note that:
- The βs are super consistent because they converge to their true values faster than OLS βs for I(0) series.
- If y_t and x_t are cointegrated there must be granger causality in at least one direction.
- 2 series of different orders of integration cannot be cointegrated.
- A linear combination of 2 I(2) series that is I(1) is cointegrated.
- A linear combination of 2 I(2) series that is I(1) can be multi-cointegrated if it is cointegrated with another I(1) series.

Cointegration Tests

2 I(1) variables y_t and x_t are cointegrated if their linear combination:

(A) $Z_{1t} = y_t - \gamma_1 - \gamma_2 x_t$

(B) $Z_{2t} = x_t - \partial_1 - \partial_2 y_t$

is white noise, I(1) and therefore stationary.

There are two main tests of cointegration.

Engle-Granger CRADF Test
A test of cointegration is the Engle-Granger Cointegrating Regression Augmented Dickey-Fuller (CRADF) test. The CRADF test has the following steps:

1) Regress the cointegrating regression $x_t = \beta_1 + \beta_2 y_t + e_t$ and save the residuals e_t.

2) Regress:

$$\Delta e_t = \alpha_1 e_{t-1} + \delta_1 \Delta e_{t-1} + \cdots \delta_m \Delta e_{t-m} + u_t$$

Autocorrelation (AC) may be present in this regression. Again, the Breusch-Godfrey (BG) test can be used to detect AC. And again the lags of Δe_t are included to eliminate any AC. m can be determined by the Schwarz-Bayesian Information Criterion or Akaike Information Criterion.

3) The null hypothesis is H_0: $\alpha = 0$, e_t is I(1), nonstationary, and the regression of x_t on y_t is spurious since they are not cointegrated. And the alternative hypothesis is H_1: $\alpha < 0$, e_t is I(0), stationary, and so x_t and y_t are cointegrated.

4) Calculate the τ_α statistic $\tau_\alpha = \frac{\alpha}{se(\alpha)}$ and obtain the CRADF critical value c for the chosen level of significance. These CRADF critical values are different from the Dickey Fuller critical values because the OLS estimation of the cointegrating regression minimizes RSS and biases the CRADF test towards finding cointegration.

5) If $|\tau_\alpha| > |c|$ then reject the null hypothesis, x_t and y_t are cointegrated. If $|\tau_\alpha| < |c|$ then do not reject the null hypothesis, x_t and y_t are not cointegrated.

6) Repeat for the other cointegrating regression of y_t on x_t.

ECM t Test
Another cointegration test is the ECM t test. Assume a 1st order ECM for simplicity:

$$\Delta y_t = \beta_1 + \beta_2 \Delta x_t + \beta_3(y_{t-1} - \gamma_1 - \gamma_2 x_{t-1}) + \varepsilon_t$$

This ECM can now be transformed into the ECM t test.

The ECM t test has the following steps:

1) Regress:

$$\Delta y_t = \beta_1^* + \beta_2 \Delta x_t + \beta_3(y_{t-1} - x_{t-1}) + \beta_4 x_{t-1} + \varepsilon_t$$

Where $\beta_1^* = \beta_1 - \beta_3 \gamma_1$ and $\beta_4 = \beta_3(1 - \gamma_2)$.

Again, AC may be present and can be detected by the BG test. If AC is present then lags of Δy_t can be added to eliminate AC.

2) The null hypothesis is $H_0: \beta_3 = 0$, x_t and y_t are cointegrated. And the alternative hypothesis is $H_1: \beta_3 < 0$, x_t and y_t are cointegrated.

3) Obtain the critical value c from the Banerjee, Dolado and Mestre table for the chosen level of significance. Note that at the 5% level of significance and for 500 degrees of freedom, the Bannerjee, Dolado and Mestre critical value is -3.23.

4) Calculate the t stat $= \frac{\beta_3}{se(\beta_3)}$.

5) If $|t| > |c|$ then reject the null hypothesis, x_t and y_t are cointegrated. If $|t| < |c|$ then do not reject the null hypothesis, x_t and y_t are not cointegrated.

6) Repeat for the other cointegrating regression of y_t on x_t.

Error Correction Models

An ECM allows us to link together the short-run dynamics and the long-run relationship between two cointegrated variables. If x_t and y_t are cointegrated, then they have a long-run equilibrium relationship where one effects the other and pulls it in the same direction overtime. An ECM builds on this and explains how shocks to x_t causes short-run disequilibrium in y_t and then how y_t subsequently adjusts back to long-run equilibrium.

Assume the long run equilibrium relationship is:

$$lnY_t = lnc + \gamma_2 lnX_t$$

or more simply:

$$y_t = \gamma_1 + \gamma_2 x_t$$

Let's start with an autoregressive distributed lag model ARDL(1,1) with two variables x_t and y_t:

$$y_t = a_0 + a_1 x_t + a_2 x_{t-1} + b y_{t-1} + u_t$$

Minus y_{t-1} from both sides:

$$y_t - y_{t-1} = a_0 + a_1 x_t + a_2 x_{t-1} + b y_{t-1} - y_{t-1} + u_t$$

Add a positive and negative $a_1 x_{t-1}$ to both sides,

$$y_t - y_{t-1} = a_0 + a_1 x_t - a_1 x_{t-1} + a_1 x_{t-1} + a_2 x_{t-1} + b y_{t-1} - y_{t-1} + u_t$$

Rewritten as:

$$\Delta y_t = a_0 + a_1 \Delta x_t + (a_1 + a_2) x_{t-1} - \lambda y_{t-1} + u_t$$

where $\lambda = (1 - b)$.

$$\Delta y_t = a_0 + a_1 \Delta x_t - \lambda(y_{t-1} - \gamma_2 x_{t-1}) + u_t$$

where $(-\lambda)(-\gamma_2) = \lambda \gamma_2 = a_1 + a_2$.

Add and minus $\lambda \gamma_1$ on the right hand side:

$$\Delta y_t = (a_0 - \lambda \gamma_1) + a_1 \Delta x_t - \lambda(y_{t-1} - \gamma_1 - \gamma_2 x_{t-1}) + u_t$$

And finally we come to the ECM equation:

$$\Delta lnY_t = \beta_1 + \beta_2 \Delta lnX_t + \beta_3 (lnY_{t-1} - \gamma_1 - \gamma_2 lnX_{t-1}) + u_t$$

Resultantly, the ECM reveals the dynamics of the relationship between X_t and Y_t by deeply exploring the adjustment process.

The part inside the brackets is the disequilibrium error, that is, the difference between the equilibrium and actual values of Y_t in the previous period.

β_3 is the adjustment coefficient, $0 > \beta_3 > -1$, it measures the speed of adjustment, or how long it takes for any disequilibrium to disappear so that Y_t reverts back to its long-run equilibrium value. Because $0 > \beta_3 > -1$, Y_t always eventually reverts back to its long-run equilibrium value after deviating from equilibrium. For example, if $(lnY_{t-1} - \gamma_1 - \gamma_2 lnX_{t-1}) > 0$, then there is positive disequilibrium because Y_t overshot its equilibrium value in the previous period, and the positive disequilibrium term falls overtime as the adjustment coefficient β_3 pushes Y_t back down to its long-run equilibrium value. And if $(lnY_{t-1} - \gamma_1 - \gamma_2 lnX_{t-1}) < 0$, then there is negative disequilibrium because Y_t undershot its equilibrium value in the previous period, and the negative disequilibrium term falls overtime as the adjustment coefficient β_3 pulls Y_t back up to its long-run equilibrium value. The smaller is β_3, the longer is the speed of adjustment. The larger is β_3, the faster is the speed of adjustment.

The short-run multiplier is simply $\frac{dy}{dx} = \gamma_2$, this is the instantaneous change in the mean of Y_t that follows a change in X_t. And the long-run multiplier is β_2, this is the absolute change in Y_t that occurs as a result of all the changes in X_t once Y_t reverts to long-run equilibrium.

Estimating Error Correction Models

There are three different ways to estimate ECMs. The Engle-Granger 2 step method, the Engle-Granger 3 step method and the unrestricted ECM method. Each gives estimates of the short run elasticity, the long run elasticity and the speed of adjustment.

Engle-Granger 2 Step Method
For the Engle-Granger 2 step method we can begin with an ECM, let's say an ECM(1) for simplicity:

$$\Delta y_t = \beta_1 + \beta_2 \Delta x_t + \beta_3(y_{t-1} - \gamma_1 - \gamma_2 x_{t-1}) + u_t$$

The Engle-Granger 2 step method has the following steps:

1) Regress the cointegrating relationship $y_t = \gamma_1 + \gamma_2 x_t$ and obtain a consistent estimate of the long run elasticity $\hat{\gamma}_2$ and obtain the residuals e_t.

2) Substitute e_t into the disequilibrium error in the ECM(1) to get:

$$\Delta y_t = \beta_1 + \beta_2 \Delta x_t + \beta_3 e_{t-1} + u_t$$

and obtain the short run elasticity $\hat{\beta}_2$ and the speed of adjustment $\hat{\beta}_3$.

Engle-Granger-Yoo 3 Step Method
The Engle-Granger-Yoo 3 step method builds on the 2 step method. In the 2 step method, the estimate $\hat{\gamma}_2$ may be biased in finite samples, so t tests are misleading. The 3 step method adjusts $\hat{\gamma}_2$ so that t tests are valid.

Engle-Granger-Yoo 3 step method has the following steps:

- All the same until midway through the 2nd step of the Engle-Granger 2 step method, now after getting $\Delta y_t = \beta_1 + \beta_2 \Delta x_t + \beta_3 e_{t-1} + u_t$ we must obtain $\hat{\beta}_3$ and $\hat{u}_t$.

3) Then create the variable $A = -\hat{\beta}_3 x_t$. Regress $\hat{u}_t = \delta_1 + \delta_2 A_{t-1} + V_t$ and obtain $\hat{\delta}_2$. Adjust the long-run elasticity such that $\hat{\gamma}_2^* = \hat{\gamma}_2 + \hat{\delta}_2$. Generate new residuals $e_t^* = y_t - \hat{\gamma}_1 - \hat{\gamma}_2^* x_t$. Regress the ECM $\Delta y_t = \theta_1 + \theta_2 \Delta x_t + \theta_3 e_{t-1}^* + w_t$ and obtain the short-run elasticity $\hat{\theta}_2$ and the speed of adjustment $\hat{\theta}_3$.

Unrestricted ECM Estimation
The unrestricted ECM estimation method transforms the ECM to allow the short-run and long-run elasticities to be obtained at the same time without having to estimate the cointegrating regression.

Unrestricted ECM method has the following steps:

1) Begin with an ECM(1) for simplicity:

$$\Delta y_t = \beta_1 + \beta_2 \Delta x_t + \beta_3(y_{t-1} - \gamma_1 - \gamma_2 x_{t-1}) + u_t$$

2) Multiply out the brackets:

$$\Delta y_t = (\beta_1 - \beta_3\gamma_1) + \beta_2\Delta x_t + \beta_3 y_{t-1} - \beta_3\gamma_2 x_{t-1} + u_t$$

3) Re-parameterize to get:

$$\Delta y_t = \beta_1^* + \beta_2\Delta x_t + \beta_3 y_{t-1} - \beta_4 x_{t-1} + u_t$$

Where $\beta_1^* = (\beta_1 - \beta_3\gamma_1)$ and $\gamma_2 = -\frac{\beta_4}{\beta_3}$.

4) Obtain the short-run elasticity $\hat{\beta}_2$, the long-run elasticity $\hat{\gamma}_2$ and the speed of adjustment $\widehat{\beta_3}$.

Note that
- For these three ECM estimation methods a higher order ECM can be modelled first, tested for HK and AC and then any insignificant variables can be dropped to leave a lower order ECM.
- Monte Carlo evidence suggests the unrestricted ECM estimators of the short-run and long-run elasticities have better small-sample properties than the Engle-Granger 2 step estimators.

Panel Data

Panel data obtains repeated observations of the same cross-sectional unit over more than one time period.

Advantages of Panel Data
- Lets us introduce unobserved heterogeneity.
- Increased information, variability, sample size, degrees of freedom and precision.
- Allows a dynamic study of regressors over time.

Let's say we have the following regression model:

$$y_{it} = \beta_0 + \delta_0 d2_t + \beta_1 X_{it} + a_i + u_{it} \quad for\ t = 1,\dots T$$

a_i is the unobserved heterogeneity or fixed effect, reflecting all unobserved time-constant factors that influence y_{it}. u_i is the idiosyncratic error term, consisting of all other time-varying factors which are not included as regressors and are also not correlated with the included regressors. Because the fixed effect is unobservable, just running a pooled OLS on the regression above leads to a kind of omitted variable bias. a_i is effectively omitted from the regression, and if a_i is endogenous then it is correlated with the included regressors and its affects are reflected in a heterogeneity bias on the regression coefficients. As a consequence, OLS estimates are no longer BLUE OLS estimates are inconsistent. The inconsistency resulting from the heterogeneity bias is mirrored by the term on the right hand side of β_1 :

$$plim\ \hat{\beta}_1^{OLS} = \beta_1 + \frac{Cov(X_{it}, a_i + u_{it})}{Var(X_{it})}$$

If $Cov(X_{it}, a_i + u_{it}) \neq 0$ then $\beta_1 \neq plim\ \hat{\beta}_1^{OLS}$ and OLS is inconsistent.

First-Differencing (FD)
First-differencing (FD) eliminates the unobserved heterogeneity by obtaining the regressors' and unobserved heterogeneity's differences between adjacent time periods. Because unobserved heterogeneity is assumed to be time-constant it will be the same in each and every time period, so its differences will equal zero and it will be differenced away from the FD regression.

Assume for simplicity that the regression model to be estimated is that of the multi-regressor and multi-time period model below:

$$y_{it} = \delta_1 + \delta_2 d2_t + \dots + \delta_T dT_t + \beta_1 X_{it1} + \dots + \beta_k X_{itk} + a_i + u_{it} \quad t = 1, \dots, T$$

FD estimation then subtracts adjacent time periods from each other to obtain the FD regression:

$$\Delta y_{it} = \delta_2 \Delta d2_t + \dots + \delta_T \Delta dT_t + \beta_1 \Delta X_{it1} + \dots + \beta_k \Delta X_{itk} + \Delta u_{it} \quad t = 2, \dots, T$$

a_i has disappeared, first-differencing has removed the unobserved heterogeneity. As long as the required assumption hold, OLS on the FD transformed regression model should yield consistent and asymptotically valid estimates.

Assumptions required for FD:
Unbiased estimates:
FD1: Regression model is linear in parameters.
FD2: Random sampling.
FD3: Each regressor is time-variant and there is no perfect multicollinearity.
FD4: $E(u_{it}|X_i, a_i) = 0$, X_{it} are strictly exogenous.
Asymptotic inferential validity:
FD5: Homoskedastic differenced idiosyncratic errors, $Var(\Delta u_{it}|X_i) = \sigma^2$ t = 2, ..., T.
FD6: No autocorrelation between differenced idiosyncratic errors, $Cov(\Delta u_{it}, \Delta u_{is}|x_i) = 0$ t≠s.
Normally distributed errors:
FD7: Δu_{it} are independently and identically distributed as $N(0, \sigma_u^2)$.

Problems with FD:
- The key strict exogeneity assumption $Cov(X_{itj}, u_{is}) = 0$ must hold.
- There must be an additive relationship between a_i and u_{it}.
- Repeated observations of the same cross sectional unit over time can be rather difficult, costly and timely to locate. Any drop-outs of observations will violate the Gauss-Markov random sampling condition.
- We lose some degrees of freedom and precision because the first observation has no antecedent.
- FD decreases the variation in the regressors so there is less explanatory power.
- Time-constant regressors are differenced away. So we cannot include dummies like gender or race.
- Autocorrelation could plague Δu_{it}.

Fixed Effects (FE)
Alternative to FD, fixed effects estimation can also remove the unobserved heterogeneity. FE removes unobserved heterogeneity by time-demeaning the variables. Assume for simplicity that the estimated regression model is the model shown below (constant has been removed for simplicity):

$$y_{it} = \beta_1 X_{it} + a_i + u_i \quad t = 1, \ldots T$$

Then the regression equation is averaged over time to get:

$$\bar{y}_i = \beta_1 \bar{X}_1 + a_i + \bar{u}_i$$

a_i is time-invariant so its mean over time is simply a_i. FE then applies within-transformation to the regression model by subtracting the time averaged regression model from the initial regression to get:

$$(y_{it} - \bar{y}_i) = \beta_1 (X_{it} - \bar{X}_1) + (a_i - a_i) + (u_i - \bar{u}_i) \quad t = 1, \ldots T$$

More importantly, it is shown that a_i has been removed:

$$\ddot{y}_{it} = \beta_1 \ddot{X}_1 + \ddot{u}_{it} \quad t = 1, \ldots T$$

Where $\ddot{y}_{it} = (y_{it} - \bar{y}_i)$, $\ddot{X}_1 = (X_{it} - \bar{X}_1)$ and $\ddot{u}_{it} = (u_i - \bar{u}_i)$.

As long as the required assumption hold, OLS on the FE within-transformed regression model will yield consistent and asymptotically valid estimates.

Assumptions required for FE:
Unbiased and consistent estimates:
FE1: Regression model is linear in parameters.
FE2: Random sampling.
FE3: Each regressor is time-variant and there is no perfect multicollinearity.
FE4: $E(u_{it}|X_i, a_i) = 0$, X_{it} are strictly exogenous.
Asymptotic inferential validity:
FE5: Homoskedastic idiosyncratic errors, $Var(u_{it}|X_i) = \sigma^2$ t = 2, …, T.
FE6: No autocorrelation between idiosyncratic errors, $Cov(u_{it}, u_{is}|X_i) = 0$ t≠s.
Normally distributed errors:
FE7: u_{it} are independently and identically distributed as $N(0, \sigma_u^2)$.

Problems with FE:
- We lose some degrees of freedom due to time-demeaning the data, N degrees of freedom are eaten up, so df = N(T-1)-k.
- Any time-constant regressor is deleted because its time-average is itself so when it is subtracted from itself it becomes zero. So we cannot include time constant dummies on their own. But we can include time-constant dummies as interaction terms if we want to increase the precision of our FE estimates.
- Requires the strict exogeneity assumption and no autocorrelation.

Random Effects (RE)
Alternative to FD and FE, if we assume that a_i is uncorrelated with the regressors, $Cov(X_{it}, a_i) = 0$ for all i and t, then RE estimation allows another route to estimating a regression model plagued with unobserved heterogeneity. RE does not need to remove the unobserved heterogeneity because of the assumption that it is uncorrelated with all regressors, but RE does need to account for the subsequent appearance of autocorrelation in the composite error term. Assume for simplicity that the regression model to be estimated is:

$$y_{it} = \beta_0 + \beta_1 X_{it1} + \cdots + \beta_k X_{itk} + a_i + u_i \quad t = 1, \ldots T$$

Because the composite error term $v_{it} = a_i + u_i$ is plagued by autocorrelation:

$$Corr(v_{it}, v_{is}) = \frac{\sigma_a^2}{(\sigma_a^2 + \sigma_u^2)} \quad for\ t \neq s$$

OLS cannot be applied directly to estimate the regression model as it would lead to inefficiency and inferential violations of test statistics.

RE estimation of the regression model instead purges the autocorrelation in the composite error term. RE requires a Generalized Least Squares (GLS) type transformation, a kind of quasi-demeaned differencing to reflect autocorrelation by applying weights of:

$$\lambda = 1\sqrt{\left(\frac{(\sigma_a^2)}{(\sigma_a^2 + T\sigma_u^2)}\right)}$$

Applying the estimated weights $\hat{\lambda}$ through Estimated Generalized Least Squares (EGLS), we get a kind of quasi-demeaned spliced weighted combination of OLS and FE:

$$(y_{it} - \hat{\lambda}\bar{y}_i) + \beta_0(1 - \hat{\lambda}) + \beta_1(X_{it1} - \hat{\lambda}\bar{X}_{it}) + \cdots + \beta_k(X_{itk} - \hat{\lambda}\bar{X}_{it}) + (v_{it} - \hat{\lambda}\bar{v}_i) \quad t=1, \ldots, T$$

As long as all the required assumptions hold, the resultant RE estimates are consistent and asymptotically normally distributed.

Assumptions required for RE:
Consistent estimates:
RE1: Regression model is linear in parameters.
RE2: Random sampling.
RE3: Regressors can be time-constant and there is no perfect multicollinearity.
RE4: $E(u_{it}|X_i, a_i) = 0$, X_{it} are strictly exogenous (conditional on the unobserved effects). Also, $Cov(X_{it}, a_i) = 0$ for all i and t.
Asymptotic inferential validity:
RE5: Homoskedastic idiosyncratic errors, $Var(u_{it}|X_i) = \sigma^2$ t = 2, ..., T. Also, homoskedastic a_i $Var(a_i|X_i) = \sigma_a^2$.
RE6: No autocorrelation between idiosyncratic errors, $cov(u_{it}, u_{is}|x_i) = 0$ t≠s.
Normally distributed errors:
RE7: u_{it} are independently and identically distributed as $N(0, \sigma_u^2)$.

RE/FE/OLS

Pooled OLS relies on a weighted average of the total sum of within variation (variation of an individual across time) and between variation (variation across different individuals).

RE relies on a different weighted average of within and between variation, where the weights reflect:

$$\lambda = 1\sqrt{\left(\frac{(\sigma_a^2)}{(\sigma_a^2 + T\sigma_u^2)}\right)}$$

FE relies just on within variation.

So:
A) As heterogeneity across individuals becomes smaller, between variation tends towards zero, FE tends towards pooled OLS.
B) As heterogeneity in the sample becomes smaller, σ_a^2 becomes smaller relative to σ_u^2, so λ tends towards zero, RE tends towards the pooled OLS estimates.
C) As heterogeneity in the sample becomes larger, σ_a^2 becomes larger relative to σ_u^2, so λ tends towards one, RE tends towards the FE estimator.

Choosing Between FD, FE and RE

FD vs. FE
Assuming FE1 through to FE4 (the same as FD1 through to FD4) and homoskedastic idiosyncratic errors, then the choice between FD and FE depends not on consistency but on relative efficiency which in turn depends on the degree of autocorrelation in the idiosyncratic errors. There are three autocorrelation situations to consider to decide which is the most efficient estimator:
A) If the idiosyncratic errors u_{it} are serially uncorrelated, then the differenced idiosyncratic errors Δu_{it} are plagued by autocorrelation since the AR(1) process of Δu_{it} has ρ equal to - ½. This can be shown as follows:
An absence of autocorrelation in u_{it} means that:

$$\text{Cov}((u_{it} - u_{it-1}),(u_{it-1} - u_{it-2})) = E((u_{it} - u_{it-1})(u_{it-1} - u_{it-2})) = E(u_{it}\,u_{it-1}) - E(u_{it}\,u_{it-2}) - E(u_{it-1}^2) + E(u_{it-1}\,u_{it-2}) = \text{zero} - \text{zero} - \sigma_u^2 + \text{zero} = -\sigma_u^2$$

And subsequently:

$$\rho = (-\sigma_u^2)/(\sqrt{\sigma_u^2} + \sqrt{\sigma_u^2}) = -\tfrac{1}{2}$$

So FE will be more efficient than FD if there is no autocorrelation between the idiosyncratic errors u_{it}.

B) If the idiosyncratic errors u_{it} follows a random walk and so are serially correlated then differenced idiosyncratic errors Δu_{it} are not plagued by autocorrelation and FD will be more efficient than FE.
C) If the AR(1) process for the idiosyncratic errors has a ρ between zero and one then it is difficult to judge on the most efficient estimator. Perhaps both FD and FE estimations can be run and compared/contrasted to look for any eye-popping substantial differences.
D) When T=2, FD and FE are identical, choose FD as it is simpler.
E) FE is better when using unbalanced data because it does not cut down the data to the shortest time series unlike FD.

RE vs. FE

All but two required assumptions are the same for RE and FE:
A) For RE, assumption FE3 is modified to RE3 by allowing there to be time-constant regressors. RE only subtracts a fraction of the time averaged time-constant variable from itself, so time-constant regressors are not deleted in RE unlike in FE where time-constant regressors are completely subtracted from themselves. This allows RE to include time-constant regressors so allows more explanatory power and diversity.
B) But as a consequence of allowing time-constant regressors to be included, RE must make an additional assumption on top of FE4. RE4 requires not only strict exogeneity $E(u_{it}|X_i, a_i) = 0$ but also $\text{Cov}(X_{it}, a_i) = 0$ for all i and t. Allowing time-constant regressors means that the unobserved heterogeneity is included in the RE estimation and if the unobserved heterogeneity is endogenous then a heterogeneity bias appears. So RE4 is compelled to make the additional assumption on top of FE4 that $\text{Cov}(X_{it}, a_i) = 0$ for all i and t. Also, introducing the unobserved heterogeneity requires RE to correct for autocorrelation in the composite error term. FE does not require this additional assumption because the unobserved heterogeneity is swept away from the regression.

Instrumental Variables

Endogeneity
A regression model may have endogenous regressors that are correlated with the error term due to unobserved heterogeneity.

$$y_i = \beta_0 + \beta_1 X + u$$

Where X is endogenous so Cov(X, u) ≠ 0.

As Cov(X, u) ≠ 0, OLS becomes inconsistent because:

$$plim\ \hat{\beta}_1^{OLS} = \beta_1 + \frac{Cov(X, u)}{Var(X)}$$

Where $\frac{Cov(X,u)}{Var(X)}$ is the asymptotic bias.

Instrumental Variable (IV)
An instrumental variable (IV) can be used to obtain consistent estimates when endogeneity arises. Let's start with the regression model:

$$y_i = \beta_0 + \beta_1 X + u$$

Where X is endogenous so Cov(X, u) ≠ 0.

An IV, denote it Z, can be used in place of X. A valid IV must:
- Be uncorrelated with u, Cov(Z, u) = 0, so that it is exogenous and does not cause inconsistency.
- Be correlated with the variable that it is representing because we want to measure the effects of that variable on the dependent variable. So Cov(Z, X) ≠ 0, Z must pick up a strong signal from X and represent it to mirror most of its variation.

So a good IV must be exogenous Cov(Z, u) = 0 and be correlated with the endogenous variable Cov(Z, X) ≠ 0.

A valid IV will give consistent estimates. Cov(Z, u) = 0 and Cov(Z, X) ≠ 0 helps to identify β_1, i.e. we can write β_1 in terms of population moments using a sample of the data.

Since:

$$Cov(Z, y) = \hat{\beta}_1^{IV} Cov(Z, X) + Cov(Z, u)$$

$$\hat{\beta}_1^{IV} = \frac{Cov(Z, y)}{Cov(Z, X)} + \frac{Cov(Z, u)}{Cov(Z, X)}$$

$$E(\hat{\beta}_1^{IV}) = \beta_1 + E\left(\frac{Cov(Z, u)}{Cov(Z, X)}\right)$$

Because X is endogenous, Cov(X, u) ≠ 0. So in small samples, $\hat{\beta}_1^{IV}$ is biased because Cov(Z, u) ≠ 0. The IV estimator is therefore biased in small samples. But in large samples, the IV estimator is consistent because Corr(Z, u)=0:

$$Plim\ \hat{\beta}_1^{IV} = \beta_1 + \frac{Corr(Z,u)}{Corr(Z,X)} \cdot \frac{\sigma_u}{\sigma_X} = \beta_1$$

And, by comparison, the OLS estimate is inconsistent because $Corr(X, u) \neq 0$:

$$Plim\ \hat{\beta}_1^{OLS} = \beta_1 + Corr(X,u) \cdot \frac{\sigma_u}{\sigma_X} \neq \beta_1$$

Multiple Regression and IV

Let's start with the structural equation:

$$y_1 = \beta_0 + \beta_1 y_2 + \beta_2 X_2 + u$$

An IV is needed for y_2 because it is endogenous.

A valid IV must still be exogenous Cov(Z, u) = 0 but now it must also have an effect on y_1 once we have controlled for the effects of X on y_1, i.e. Z must have partial effects on y_1. So in the reduced form equation (the regression of the endogenous variable y_2 on all the exogenous variables and Z):

$$y_2 = \pi_0 + \pi_1 X + \pi_2 Z + v$$

π_2 must be statistically different from zero. We can easily test this with a t test with $H_0: \pi_2 = 0$ and $H_1: \pi_2 \neq 0$. If we reject the null hypothesis then Z does have partial correlation with y_2 so we can use Z in place of y_2. And as long as Z is also exogenous Cov(Z, u) = 0 then Z is a good IV and gives consistent estimates.

2 Stage Least Squares (2SLS)

We use 2 Stage Least Squares (2SLS) when we have multiple IVs for the same endogenous variable i.e. we have Z_1, Z_2, Z_3 etc to act as instruments. We could just pick one of the IVs and use that one on its own or we could use 2SLS to find the best linear combination of the instruments to replace X.

Let's start with:

$$y_1 = \beta_0 + \beta_1 y_2 + \beta_2 X_2 + u$$

Where y_2 is endogenous and X is exogenous in the structural equation.

Let's say the exclusion restriction is that the IVs Z_1 and Z_2 are not included in the structural equation and they are both exogenous.

We now use 2SLS to get the linear combination of IVs that is most correlated with y_2.

2SLS steps:

1) Estimate the best linear combination $y_2^* = \pi_0 + \pi_1 X + \pi_2 Z_1 + \pi_3 Z_2$ and obtain the fitted values $\hat{y}_2^*$.

2) Regress y_1 on $\hat{y}_2^*$ and X:

$$y_1 = \beta_0 + \beta_1^{IV} \hat{y}_2^* + \beta_2 X$$

And β_1^{IV} gives us a consistent estimator.

Both Z_1 and Z_2 must not appear in the structural equation, both must be exogenous Cov(Z_1, u) = 0 and Cov(Z_2, u) = 0 and at least one must have some partial effect on y_1 for their linear combination to be a valid instrument.

Note: The order condition is necessary for consistency of IV estimates. The order condition is: we must have at least as many IVs as we have endogenous regressors in our structural equation.

Poor Instruments
Instruments may be poor. Consider the following:

High Asymptotic Variance
A valid IV gives higher standard errors than an OLS estimator. IVs have an asymptotic normal distribution and the asymptotic variance of IV estimators converge to zero at the rate 1/n like OLS. But, IV estimators always have a larger asymptotic variance than OLS estimators. This is because:

$$Asymptotic\ Variance\ of\ \hat{\beta}_1^{IV} = \frac{\hat{\sigma}^2}{TSS_X \cdot R_{X,Z}^2}$$

$$Asymptotic\ Variance\ of\ \hat{\beta}_1^{OLS} = \frac{\hat{\sigma}^2}{TSS_X}$$

$R_{X,Z}^2$ is the R^2 from an auxiliary regression of X on the IV Z. Because $R_{X,Z}^2 < 1$, if X is not Z then the $\hat{\beta}_1^{IV}$ estimator has a larger asymptotic variance than $\hat{\beta}_1^{OLS}$.

Note, the weaker is Z as an IV, the less variation of X it mirrors and thus the lower is $R_{X,Z}^2$. As $R_{X,Z}^2$ falls, the asymptotic variance of $\hat{\beta}_1^{IV}$ relative to $\hat{\beta}_1^{OLS}$ increases a lot and there is an even larger sampling variance for $\hat{\beta}_1^{IV}$.

Also note that, if we are using a multiple regression, multicollinearity could plague the instruments and make the asymptotic variance of $\hat{\beta}_1^{IV}$ even larger.

The asymptotic variance of $\hat{\beta}_1^{IV}$ in a multiple regression is:

$$\hat{\beta}_1^{IV} = \frac{\hat{\sigma}^2}{TSS_{y_2}(1 - \hat{R}_{y_2}^2)}$$

$\hat{R}_{y_2}^2$ is the R^2 from a regression of the best linear combination IV $\hat{y}_2$ on all other exogenous variables in the structural equation. Because a regression of $\hat{y}_2$ on all the exogenous variables in the structural equation will have a higher R^2 than a regression of y_2 on all the exogenous variables in the structural equation, 2SLS IV estimators will have an even higher asymptotic variance than OLS estimators.

Asymptotic Bias

$$Plim\ \hat{\beta}_1^{IV} = \beta_1 + \frac{Corr(Z,u)}{Corr(Z,X)} \cdot \frac{\sigma_u}{\sigma_X}$$

$$Plim\ \hat{\beta}_1^{OLS} = \beta_1 + Corr(X,u) \cdot \frac{\sigma_u}{\sigma_X}$$

OLS might be more consistent than IV if $\frac{Corr(Z,u)}{Corr(Z,X)} > Corr(X,u)$.

As Z becomes a worse IV, the less variation of X it mirrors, the lower is Corr(Z, X) and thus the higher is the asymptotic bias.

Negative R^2

An IV can give a negative R^2. $R^2 = 1 - \frac{RSS}{TSS}$ and for IVs, RSS can be > TSS so R^2 can be negative. However, we do not use the R^2 from IV, we only use IV to give consistency. And anyway, when we have an endogenous regressor we cannot even decompose the variance of y into $\beta_1^2 Var(X) + Var(u)$ so the R^2 for OLS has no natural interpretation to compare to the IV R^2.

Logit and Probit Models

The Linear Probability Model (LPM)

Let's look at the Linear Probability Model (LPM):

$$y_i = X_i\beta + u_i$$

y_i is a binary outcome and follows a Bernoulli distribution: either $y_i = 1$ with probability P_i or $y_i = 0$ with probability $1 - P_i$.

y_i	Probability
1	P_i
0	$1 - P_i$
Total	1

So our model becomes:

$$E(y|X) = X_i\beta = P(y = 1|X) = P_i$$

Shortcomings of the LPM

Let's look at the slope coefficient of the LPM:

$$\Delta P(y = 1|X) = \beta_j \Delta X_j$$

β_j measures the change in the probability of success y=1 when X increases by 1 unit. Because the response probability $P(y = 1|X)$ depends on some linear function of X_j, there is always the same constant marginal effect, for example, if X increases from a small value or from a high value it will always have the same marginal effect on $P(y = 1|X)$. So the LPM does not let us explain decreasing marginal returns.

The biggest problem is that the LMP can predict probabilities that are less than zero or greater than one. This is impossible though, for example, we cannot say that there is a -10% chance or a 120% chance of a player scoring a goal in a football game. The LPM can work well for value for X close to the mean but it does not work well when it predicts probabilities that are less than zero or greater than one.

LPM and Impossible Probabilities

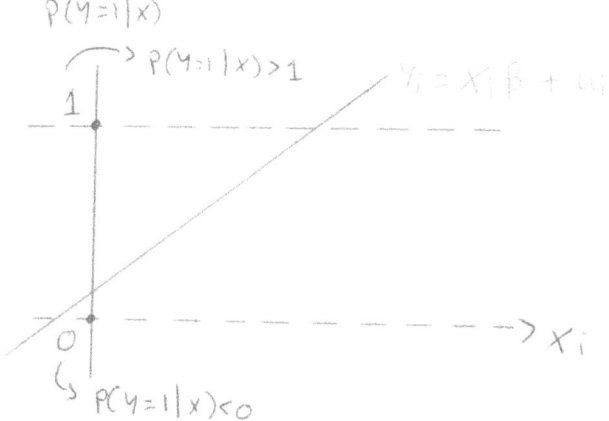

Consequences of Estimating LPM by OLS

Many negative consequences arise if the LPM is estimated by OLS including:

1) OLS may lead to a low R^2 because the linear function does not really cross through all the scattered data.

LPM, OLS and Low R^2

But note, we can use another R^2, the per cent correctly predicted.

2) As y_i follows a Bernoulli distribution, u_i will too and thus will not be normally distributed, so our OLS estimates will give invalid t stats and therefore our inferential tests will be violated.

$$u_i = y_i - \beta_i X_i$$

y_i	u_i	Probability
$y_i = 1$	$1 - \beta_i X_i$	P_i
$y_i = 0$	$-\beta_i X_i$	$1 - P_i$

But note, as the sample size increases indefinitely, we can rely on the Central Limit Theorem so that u is asymptotically normally distributed.

3) The biggest problem is that there is heteroskedasticity (HK) in the LPM and OLS does not account for this so our inferential statements from OLS test statistics will be invalid. Even if $E(u_i) = 0$ and $Cov(u_i, u_j) = 0 \ for \ i \neq j$, there will still be HK because:

$$Var(y_i|X) = P_i(1 - P_i) = (\beta_i X_i)(-\beta_i X_i)$$

So $(y_i|X)$ depends on X_i and is not constant so there is HK.

But note, we can use Weighted Least Squares to solve the HK problem.

Logit and Probit Models

Logit and Probit models can be used instead of the LPM. We can use a nonlinear function to model the response probability.

$$P(y = 1|X) = (G(\beta X_i))$$

Where 0<G(Z)<1 and Z are all real numbers.

Logit Model

In the Logit model, G is the logistic function:

$$G(Z) = \frac{\exp Z}{1 + \exp Z} = \Lambda(Z)$$

Where $0 < \Lambda(Z) < 1$ for all real numbers Z.

Probit Model

In the Probit model, G is the standard normal cumulative distribution function:

$$G(Z) = \int_{-\infty}^{Z} \phi(V) dV = \Phi(Z)$$

Where ϕ is the standard normal density, $\phi(Z) = (2\pi)^{-\frac{1}{2}} \exp\left(\frac{-Z^2}{2}\right)$, and $0 < \Phi(Z) < 1$ for all real numbers Z.

For both the Logit and Probit models:

$$G(Z) \rightarrow 0 \text{ as } Z \rightarrow -\infty$$

And:

$$G(Z) \rightarrow 1 \text{ as } Z \rightarrow \infty$$

Bounded Probabilities

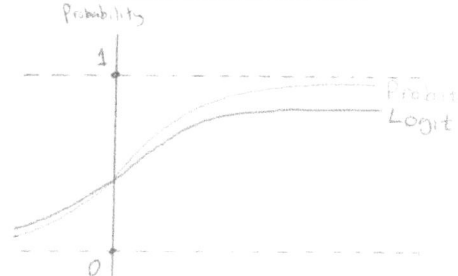

So the probabilities are bounded by 0 and 1 and Logit and Probit models do not give implausible probabilities like the LPM. The tails do not go above 1 or below 0 for Logit and Probit's distributions.

Deriving Logit and Probit Models from a Latent Variable
We can derive Logit and Probit models from a latent variable model. Let y* denote the latent variable.

$$y* = \beta_o + X\beta + e$$

Where $y = 1$ $(Y* > 0)$ and $y = 0$ $(y* \leq 0)$.

$$P(y=1|X) = P(y* > 0|X) = P(e > -(\beta_o + X\beta)|X) = 1 - G(-(\beta_o + X\beta)) = G(\beta_o + X\beta)$$

And we specify $G(\cdot)$ as the logistic function for Logit models or the standard normal cumulative distribution function for Probit models.

Partial Effects

Because $G(\cdot)$ is nonlinear and X_j is roughly a continuous random variable, we must use calculus to determine the partial effects of X_j on $P(y = 1|X)$:

$$\frac{\delta P(y=1|X)}{\delta X_j} = g(\beta_o + X\beta)\beta_j$$

Where $g(Z) = \frac{dG}{dZ}(Z)$.

Therefore we get different marginal effects, not constant like the LPM. $G(\cdot)$ is strictly increasing so $g(Z) > 0$ for all Z.

Estimating Logit and Probit Models

We cannot use OLS on Logit and Probit models as they are nonlinear. So we must use Maximum Likelihood Estimation (MLE) instead. MLE is based on the distribution of y given X, so HK is accounted for and not a problem.

MLE will give us consistent, asymptotically normal and asymptotically efficient estimators, so we can make valid inferential statements.

For MLE we must first take the density of y_i given X_i:

$$f(y|X_i\beta) = [G(X_i\beta)]^y [1 - G(X_i\beta)]^{1-y} \quad y = 0,1$$

If y = 1 then:

$$f(\cdot) = G(X_i\beta)$$

And if y = 0 then:

$$f(\cdot) = 1 - G(X_i\beta)$$

The Log-Likelihood function for observation i is a function of the parameters and data so is obtained by the log of the above density function:

$$\mathcal{L}_i(\beta) = y_i \log[G(X_i\beta)] + (1 - y_i)\log[1 - G(X_i\beta)]$$

Then using the sample size n:

$$\mathcal{L}(\beta) = \sum_{i-1}^{n} \mathcal{L}_i(\beta)$$

And $\hat{\beta}^{MLE}$ maximizes $\mathcal{L}(\beta)$. $\hat{\beta}^{MLE}$, the MLE estimates, are the parameters which generate the observed data the most.

Again, we choose G(·) as the standard Logit or standard normal cumulative distribution function for $\hat{\beta}_{Logit}^{MLE}$ and $\hat{\beta}_{Probit}^{MLE}$ respectively.

Testing Multiple Hypotheses
The likelihood ratio (LR) test can be used to test multiple exclusion restrictions in Logit and Probit models. LR tests if $\mathcal{L}(\beta)$ becomes significantly smaller when we drop some variables as part of our restrictions.

The LR test has the following steps:

1) Estimate the unrestricted model, estimate $\mathcal{L}_{ur}$.

2) Estimate the restricted model, estimate $\mathcal{L}_r$.

3) H_o: The restrictions are valid.

    H_1: The restrictions are invalid.

4) Set up the test statistic:

$$LR = 2(\mathcal{L}_{ur} - \mathcal{L}_r) \sim X_2^2$$

5) If LR is greater than the chi-square critical value at the chosen level of significance then reject the null hypothesis, the restrictions are invalid.

Logit and Probit Goodness of Fit
We can compare the overall explanatory power of Logit and Probit models by a pseudo R^2:

$$pseudo\ R^2 = 1 - \frac{\mathcal{L}_{ur}}{\mathcal{L}_r}$$

Where $\mathcal{L}_{ur}$ is for all the explanatory variables and $\mathcal{L}_r$ is for no explanatory varibles.

Note, we could also compare their 'per cent correctly predicted'.

Comparing the LMP, Logit Models and Probit Models
Logit models have a smaller 'largest effect' than Probit models:

Logit and Probit Distributions

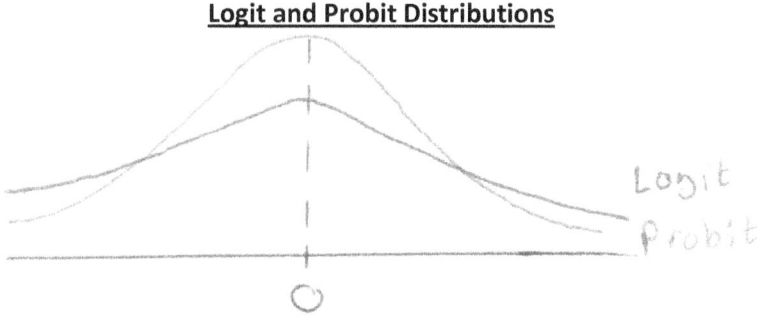

The largest effect in the LPM is $g(0) = 1$.
The largest effect in the Logit model is $g(0) = \frac{\exp(0)}{(1+\exp(0))^2} = 0.25$.
The largest effect in the Probit model is $g(0) = 0.4$.

So, to compare the magnitudes of the partial effects of all the different models we must multiply them by their respective scale factors. So to compare Logit models and Probit models to the LPM we must multiply Logit estimates by 0.25 and multiply Probit estimates by 0.4. Then all three models are comparable.

Sample Selection Bias

Let's start with the population model:

$$y = \beta_0 + \beta_1 X_1 + \cdots + \beta_k X_k + u$$

Where $E(u|X_1, \ldots, X_k) = 0$.

And our population model is for a random draw:

$$y_i = X_i \beta + u_i$$

Let's say the selection indicator is S. If Si = 1 we observe all the data for that i (y_i, X_i) and we include that i in our regression. If Si = 0 we observe no data for that i and do not include that i in our regression. So our regression model becomes:

$$S_i y_i = S_i X_i \beta + S_i u_i$$

If Si = 1 we observe the data so $y_i = X_i \beta + u_i$. If Si = 0 we do not observe the data so we get 0 = 0 + 0 = 0.

As long as as Si is determined by exogenous variables then we have an exogenous sample and OLS does not have a sample selection bias so OLS is unbiased and consistent. If all the regressors are exogenous and Si depends on them then SX_j is just a function of exogenous variables and so it is exogenously determined. So we get:

$$E(S_i u_i | S_i X_i) = S_i E(u_i | S_i X_i) = E(u_i | X_i) = 0$$

And so:

$$E(S_i y_i) = E(S_i X_i \beta) + E(S_i u_i)$$

And thus:

$$E(y_i) = X_i \beta$$

So OLS is unbiased.

And if Si is dependent on variables that are not in our regression but on ones that are independent of the regressors and u_i then Si is independent of (X_i, u_i) so $E(SX_j u) = E(S)E(X_j u) = 0$ because $E(X_j u) = 0$ and OLS is still unbiased.

As long as Si depends on exogenous variables, OLS is unbiased.

Truncated Regression

In a truncated regression mode, we do not observe some data, a subset of the population are excluded from the regression.

Let's start with:

$$y_i = \beta_o + \beta_i X_i + u_i$$

Where $u_i | X_i \sim N(0, \sigma^2)$.

If there is random sampling then OLS is consistent and efficient. A regression model that is truncated is not random. Let's say a random draw (X_i, y_i) from the population is only observed if $y_i \leq C_i$, where C_i is the truncation threshold which can depend on X_i. So our regression excludes a subset of the population based on y_i. In this case, our selectivity indicator Si depends on an endogenous variable y_i. If $y_i \leq C_i$ then Si = 1 and we observe the data for that i. If $y_i > C_i$ then we do not include that i as Si = 0 and the data is excluded from our regression. Our data is 'top-coded', we do not observe the data that is above C_i because they are excluded. Therefore, the mean of u_i is less than zero. So we have:

$$E(y_i | X_i, S_i = 1) = \beta_o + \beta_1 X_i + E(u_i | X_i, S_i = 1)$$

And because:

$$E(u_i | S_i = 1) = E(u_i | y_i < C) = E(u_i | \beta_o + \beta_1 X_i + u_i < C) = E(u_i | u_i < C - \beta_o + \beta_1 X_i) \neq 0$$
$$= F(X)$$

then:

$$E(u_i | X_i, S_i = 1) \neq 0 = F(X)$$

So OLS gives biased estimators if we use the truncated data because:

$$E(y_i | X_i, S_i = 1) = \beta_o + \beta_1 X_i + F(X)$$

Where F(X) is the bias.

Also, OLS will be inconsistent. And if we have top-coded data then our truncated regression line is flatter than the true regression line because we miss the data that is above C_i, so our OLS estimators are biased towards zero in larger samples.

Top-Coded and Inconsistency

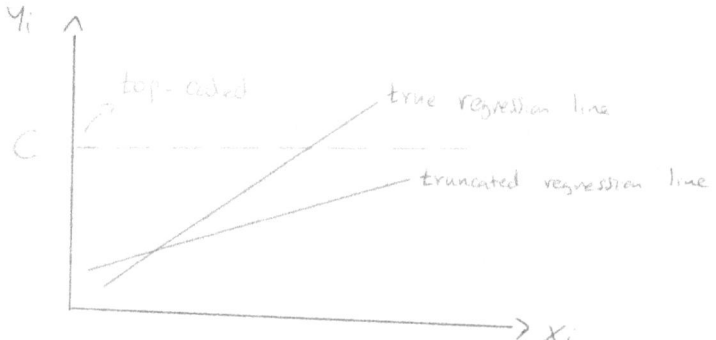

Because of truncation, the mean of y is not the same as if we have all the data to observe. So we must re-normalize the density function. We simply get the normal density function $f(y | \beta_1 X_i, \sigma^2)$ that we have when $y_i \leq C_i$ and divide it by the normal cumulative density function (CDF) $F(C_i | \beta_1 X_i, \sigma^2)$ which is basically the probability that $y_i \leq C_i$:

$$g(y|X_i, C_i) = \frac{f(y|\beta_1 X_i, \sigma^2)}{F(C_i|\beta_1 X_i, \sigma^2)}, y \leq C_i$$

And then we can obtain consistent estimators by taking the Log of the density function and get the Maximum Likelihood Estimation (MLE) estimators from:

$$\mathcal{L}(\beta, \sigma) = \prod_{i=1}^{n} \left(\frac{f(y|\beta_1 X_i, \sigma^2)}{F(C_i|\beta_1 X_i, \sigma^2)} \right)$$

An Example of Self Selection Bias in the Labour Market and the Heckit Procedure

A self selection bias problem arises out of incidental truncation. Random sampling is required for OLS estimators to be unbiased. But incidental truncation causes our estimators to become biased and inconsistent. Looking at women and their wages in the labour market, there may be a self selection bias problem because wage depends on another variable 'in the labour force' (inlf). For women who are in the labour force, where inlf = 1, their wage offer is observable because it is the wage they are being paid. But for women who are not in the labour force, where inlf = 0, their wage offer is undeterminable because they are out of work so are not being paid a wage that we can observe. So we are missing the wage data on those women who are not in the labour force. Random sampling is violated because we are missing the values of wage for women who are not in the labour force. OLS will be biased because if it misses the wage data for women who are out of the labour force then it will omit those women from the regression. But crucially we still observe all other information for these women, so we can use the Heckit procedure to consistently estimate the regression's coefficients.

Let's say the population regression model is:

$$y = X\beta + u$$

And the selection function is:

$$S = 1[Z\gamma + v \geq 0]$$

If we observe y then S = 1, if we do not observe y then S = 0. All elements of X and Z are always observed. Z is exogenous $E(u|X, Z) = 0$, X is a strict subset of Z and v is independent of Z and X. So:

$$E(y|X, Z) = X\beta + E(u|X, Z) = E(u|v) = X\beta + pv$$

Where p is the correlation coefficient between u and v.

And since v is unobservable, we rewrite this as:

$$E(y|Z, S) = X\beta + p\lambda(Z\gamma)$$

Where $\lambda(Z\gamma)$ is the inverse Mills ratio.

As long as we include $p\lambda(Z\gamma)$ then we get consistent estimates by only using the observable sample of y. OLS does not include $p\lambda(Z\gamma)$ though. If Cov(u, v) = 0 then p = 0 and OLS is consistent. But if Cov(u, v) ≠ 0 then p ≠ 0, OLS omits a relevant regressor and thus OLS is biased and inconsistent.

We must first estimate $p\lambda(Z\gamma)$ though, this is what the Heckit procedure does:

A) Use the entire sample and estimate a Probit model $P(S = 1|Z) = \emptyset(Z\gamma)$ of Si on Zi, obtain $\hat{\gamma}$ and compute $\hat{\lambda}_i = \lambda(Z_i\hat{\gamma})$.

B) With the selected sample, regress y_i on X_i and the estimated inverse Mills ratio $\hat{\lambda}_i$. And now we get consistent estimates of β.

Appendix A

Appendix A presents the OLS model, multicollinearity, heteroskedasticity and autocorrelation in matrix form.

Ordinary Least Squares (OLS)

Ordinary Least Squares (OLS) is a regression technique to estimate a linear relationship between two or more variables. Let's say we have the population regression function (PRF):

$$y = X\beta + u$$

The PRF shows the true relationship between the variables. A PRF measures how the average of Y responds to a change in X. Based on a sample of the population, OLS estimates the sample regression function (SRF):

$$y = X\hat{\beta} + \hat{u}$$

OLS: PRF and SRF

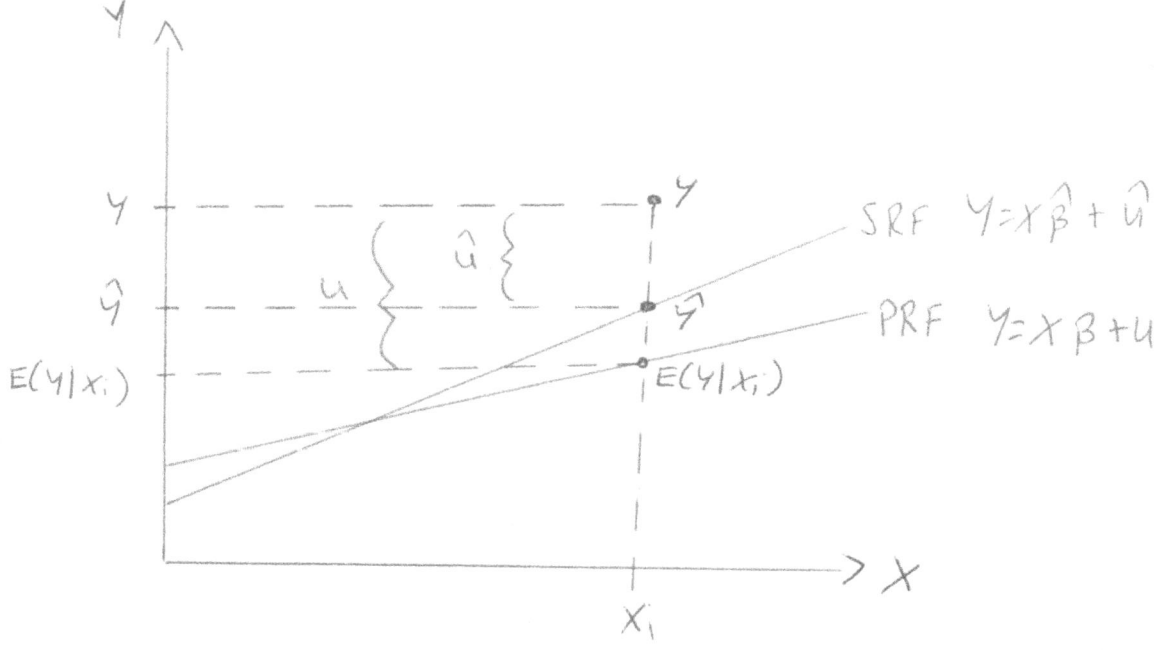

The SRF approximates the PRF. OLS estimates the PRF by minimizing the residual sum of squares (RSS). By minimizing RSS, OLS equally weights both positive and negative residuals. OLS minimizes an absolute value of the residuals and therefore approximates the SRF as close as possible to the PRF.

$$y = X\hat{\beta} + \hat{u}$$

$$\hat{y} = X\hat{\beta}$$

$$y = \hat{y} + \hat{u}$$

$$\hat{u} = y - \hat{y}$$

$$RSS = \sum \hat{u}^2 = \sum (y - \hat{y})^2$$

Classical Linear Regression Model (CLRM)
OLS relies on the assumptions of the Classical Linear Regression Model (CLRM):

Assumptions of the Regressors (X):
A.1) X is nonstochastic, it takes values determined by the researcher.
A.2) X is fixed in repeated sampling.
A.3) As the sample size (n) approaches ∞, Var(X) is finite and constant.
A.4) The Rank of $\underset{nxk}{X}$ P(X) = k, the columns of the $\underset{nxk}{X}$ matrix are linearly independent, that is, there is no multicollinearity.

Assumptions of the Residuals (u):
B.1) The expected value of the residuals equals zero, that is, E(u) = 0, so the random error term does not systematically affect the mean of Y.
B.2) $Var(u) = E(uu') = \sigma^2$, there is homoskedastic variance of u. So all Y are equally important, equally reliable and deviate from their mean by the same extent.
B.3) No autocorrelation, $Cov(u_i, u_j) = E\left((u_i - E(u_i))(u_j - E(u_j))\right) = E(u_i u_j) = 0$ for $i \neq j$.

Basically, B.2 and B.3 mean:

$$E(uu') = \begin{bmatrix} E(u^2) & E(u_1 u_2) & \dots & E(u_1 u_n) \\ E(u_2 u_1) & E(U_2^2) & \dots & E(u_2 u_n) \\ \vdots & \vdots & \ddots & \vdots \\ E(u_n u_1) & E(u_n u_2) & \dots & E(u_n^2) \end{bmatrix} = \begin{bmatrix} \sigma^2 & 0 & \dots & 0 \\ 0 & \sigma^2 & \dots & 0 \\ \vdots & \vdots & \ddots & \vdots \\ 0 & 0 & \dots & \sigma^2 \end{bmatrix} = \sigma^2$$

Where the σ^2 in the diagonal means homoskedasticity and the zeros mean no autocorrelation.

Additional Assumptions:
C.1) Correct model specification, for example, no omitted variables bias.
C.2) The sample size n is greater than the number of parameters k.
C.3) The regression model is linear in parameters, for example, β not β^2.

The Normal Equations
OLS estimates $\hat{\beta}$ by minimizing the RSS and then partially differentiating it by $\hat{\beta}$.

Given the SRF:
$$y = X\hat{\beta} + \hat{u}$$

$$\hat{u} = y - X\hat{\beta}$$

$$\hat{u}' = (y - X\hat{\beta})'$$

RSS is given by:
$$\hat{u}'\hat{u}$$

So OLS derives $\hat{\beta}$ by:
$$\hat{u}'\hat{u} = (y - X\hat{\beta})'(y - X\hat{\beta})$$

$$\hat{u}'\hat{u} = y'y - 2\hat{\beta}'X'y + \hat{\beta}'(X'X)\hat{\beta}$$

$$\frac{\partial(\hat{u}'\hat{u})}{\partial(\hat{\beta})} = -2X'y + 2(X'X)\hat{\beta} = 0$$

$$\frac{\partial(\hat{u}'\hat{u})}{\partial(\hat{\beta})} = 2(X'X)\hat{\beta} = 2X'y$$

$$\frac{\partial(\hat{u}'\hat{u})}{\partial(\hat{\beta})} = (X'X)\hat{\beta} = X'y$$

$$\frac{\partial(\hat{u}'\hat{u})}{\partial(\hat{\beta})} = (X'X)^{-1}(X'X)\hat{\beta} = (X'X)^{-1}X'y$$

$$\frac{\partial(\hat{u}'\hat{u})}{\partial(\hat{\beta})} = \hat{\beta} = (X'X)^{-1}X'y$$

The Variance of $\hat{\beta}$

The variance of $\hat{\beta}$ is derived by:

$$Var(\hat{\beta}) = E(\hat{\beta} - \beta)(\hat{\beta} - \beta)'$$

Substitute in $\hat{\beta} - \beta = (X'X)^{-1} X'u$ to get:

$$Var(\hat{\beta}) = E((X'X)^{-1} X'u)((X'X)^{-1} X'u)'$$

And since (ABC)' = C'B'A', we get:

$$Var(\hat{\beta}) = E((X'X)^{-1} X'u)(u'X(X'X)^{-1})$$

Assuming (A.1) X is nonstochastic and (A.2) X is fixed in repeated sampling, then:

$$Var(\hat{\beta}) = (X'X)^{-1} X'E(uu')X(X'X)^{-1}$$

Assuming (B.2) no heteroskedasticity and (B.3) no autocorrelation, then E(uu') = σ^2, so:

$$Var(\hat{\beta}) = (X'X)^{-1} X'\sigma^2 X(X'X)^{-1}$$

$$Var(\hat{\beta}) = \sigma^2 (X'X)^{-1} (X'X)(X'X)^{-1}$$

$$Var(\hat{\beta}) = \sigma^2 (X'X)^{-1}$$

Best Linear Unbiased Estimator (BLUE)

Assuming the Gauss-Markov conditions (A.1) X is nonstochastic, (A.2) X is fixed in repeated sampling, (B.1) E(u) = 0, (B.2) no heteroskedasticity and (B.3) no autocorrelation then the OLS estimators are best linear unbiased estimators (BLUE) in small samples.

Linear
The OLS estimator is:

$$\hat{\beta} = (X'X)^{-1}X'y$$

Assuming (A.1) X is nonstochastic and (A.2) X is fixed in repeated sampling then:

$$\hat{B} = Cy$$

C is a matrix of fixed constants:

$$\begin{bmatrix} \widehat{\beta_1} \\ \widehat{\beta_2} \\ \vdots \\ \widehat{\beta_k} \end{bmatrix} = \begin{bmatrix} C_{11} & C_{12} & \cdots & C_{1n} \\ C_{21} & C_{22} & \cdots & C_{2n} \\ \vdots & \vdots & \ddots & \vdots \\ C_{k1} & C_{k2} & \cdots & C_{kn} \end{bmatrix} = \begin{bmatrix} y_1 \\ y_2 \\ \vdots \\ y_n \end{bmatrix}$$
$$kx1 \qquad\qquad\qquad kxn \qquad\qquad\qquad 1xn$$

So $\hat{\beta}$ is linear because it is a linear function of the sample observations y.

Best and Unbiased
$\hat{\beta}$ is best because it has minimum variance amongst all other linear estimators.

$\hat{\beta}$ is unbiased since E($\hat{\beta}$) = β

Best and Unbiased

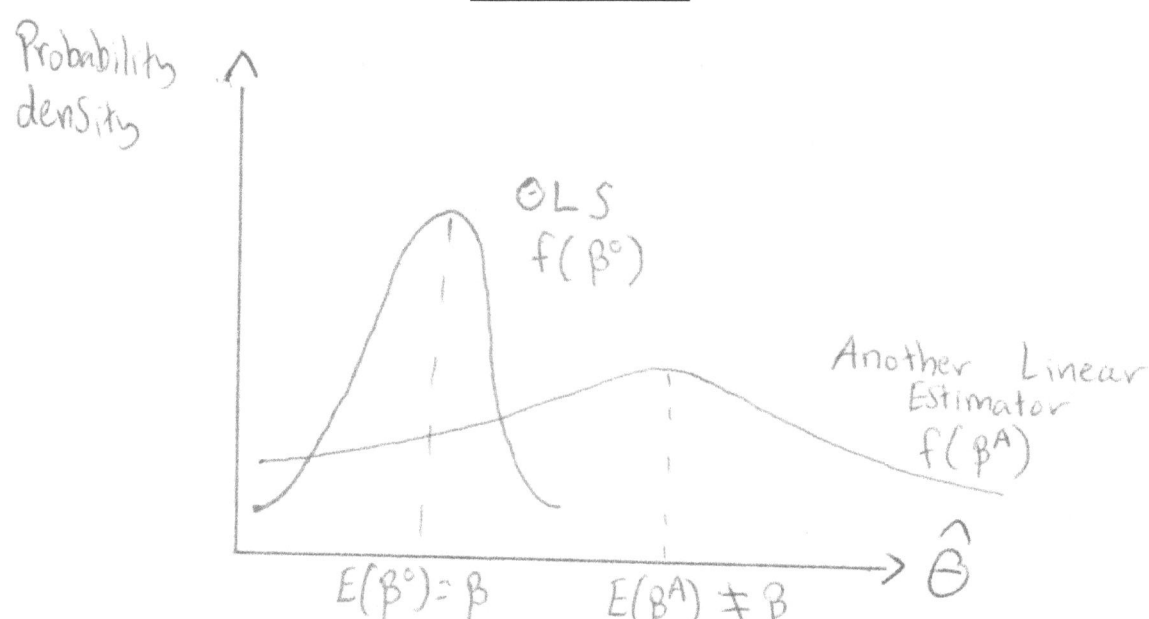

Proof of $\hat{\beta}$ Unbiasedness
The OLS estimator is:
$$\hat{\beta} = (X'X)^{-1}X'y$$

Substitute in the PRF $y = X\beta + u$ to get:
$$\hat{\beta} = (X'X)^{-1}X'(X\beta + u)$$
$$\hat{\beta} = (X'X)^{-1}(X'X)\beta + (X'X)^{-1}X'u$$
$$\hat{\beta} = \beta + (X'X)^{-1}X'u$$

Now taking the expectations:
$$E(\hat{\beta}) = E(\beta) + E((X'X)^{-1}X'u)$$

Assuming (A.1) X is nonstochastic and (A.2) X is fixed in repeated sampling then:
$$E(\hat{\beta}) = \beta + (X'X)^{-1}X'E(u)$$

And assuming (B.1) E(u) = 0 then $(X'X)^{-1}X'E(u)$ so:
$$E(\hat{\beta}) = \beta$$

Multicollinearity (MC)
Perfect MC
If there is perfect MC then OLS cannot even estimate our βs. The OLS estimator is:
$$(X'X)^{-1}\hat{\beta} = X'y$$

With perfect MC, the rank of X P(X) < k so (X'X) is singular and its inverse does not exist, so we cannot get:
$$\hat{\beta} = (X'X)^{-1}X'y$$

So OLS estimation of $\hat{\beta}$ is impossible.

Imperfect MC
If there is imperfect multicollinearity then the Var($\hat{\beta}$) and s.e.($\hat{\beta}$) become large and our inferential tests become invalid. Although, it must be noted that OLS remains BLUE if there is imperfect MC (so long as the other Gauss-Markov conditions hold). With imperfect MC, a column of X is highly correlated with another column of X so (X'X) is close to being singular, thus |X'X| is close to being zero so $(X'X)^{-1}$ is large because:
$$(X'X)^{-1} = \frac{c'}{|X'X|}$$

Where c' is the transpose of the cofactor matrix.

And if $(X'X)^{-1}$ is large then $Var(\hat{\beta}) = \sigma^2 (X'X)^{-1}$ is large.

Because $= \frac{\hat{\beta}_j - \beta_{null}}{s.e.(\hat{\beta})}$, as MC increases, our regressors become even more correlated, s.e.($\hat{\beta}$) rises, the t stat falls and becomes less significant so there is an increased chance of making a type 2 error (accepting a false null hypothesis). Because our t stats are invalidated, we may conclude that the $\hat{\beta}s$ are individually insignificant even though they are collectively significant because of a high R^2.

Heteroskedasticity (HK)
Heteroskedasticity (HK) infects the variances of OLS estimates, OLS is no longer BLUE. It is the Weighted Least Squares (WLS) estimates that are BLUE when HK is present.

Let's look at the OLS variance of $\hat{\beta}$:

$$Var(\hat{\beta}) = E(\hat{\beta} - \beta)(\hat{\beta} - \beta)'$$

Substitute in $\hat{\beta} - \beta = (X'X)^{-1} X'u$ to get:

$$Var(\hat{\beta}) = E((X'X)^{-1} X'u)((X'X)^{-1} X'u)'$$

And since (ABC)' = C'B'A', we get:

$$Var(\hat{\beta}) = E((X'X)^{-1} X'u)(u'X(X'X)^{-1})$$

Assuming (A.1) X is nonstochastic and (A.2) X is fixed in repeated sampling, then:

$$Var(\hat{\beta}) = (X'X)^{-1} X'E(uu')X(X'X)^{-1}$$

Assuming (B.2) no HK and (B.3) no autocorrelation, then E(uu') = σ^2, so:

$$Var(\hat{\beta}) = (X'X)^{-1} X'\sigma^2 X(X'X)^{-1}$$

$$Var(\hat{\beta}) = \sigma^2 (X'X)^{-1} (X'X)(X'X)^{-1}$$

$$Var(\hat{\beta}) = \sigma^2 (X'X)^{-1}$$

However, if there is HK then $E(uu') \neq \sigma^2 = V$ so:

$$Var(\hat{\beta}) = (X'X)^{-1} X'VX(X'X)^{-1}$$

So HK causes t tests to become invalid. Monte Carlo experiments show that, when OLS is infected by HK and takes into account HK, OLS variances are biased upwards, OLS standard errors are biased upwards and thus OLS t stats are biased downwards. So under OLS, there is an increased chance of making a type 2 error, $\hat{\beta}$ may be wrongly concluded to be insignificant when it is actually significant under the BLUE WLS.

Autocorrelation (AC)
Autocorrelation (AC) infects the variances of OLS estimates and causes inferential statements to become invalid, OLS is no longer BLUE.

AC means $\sigma_{ij} \neq 0$ for $i \neq j$ so:

$$E(uu') = \begin{bmatrix} \sigma^2 & \sigma_{12} & \cdots & \sigma_{1n} \\ \sigma_{21} & \sigma^2 & \cdots & \sigma_{2n} \\ \vdots & \vdots & \ddots & \vdots \\ \sigma_{n1} & \sigma_{n2} & \cdots & \sigma^2 \end{bmatrix}$$

Let's say u_t follows an AR(1) scheme:

$$u_t = pu_{t-1} + \varepsilon_t$$

Where ε_t is white noise.

Let's look at the OLS variance of $\hat{\beta}$:

$$Var(\hat{\beta}) = E(\hat{\beta} - \beta)(\hat{\beta} - \beta)'$$

Substitute in $\hat{\beta} - \beta = (X'X)^{-1} X'u$ to get:

$$Var(\hat{\beta}) = E((X'X)^{-1} X'u)((X'X)^{-1} X'u)'$$

And since (ABC)' = C'B'A', we get:

$$Var(\hat{\beta}) = E((X'X)^{-1} X'u)(u'X(X'X)^{-1})$$

Assuming (A.1) X is nonstochastic and (A.2) X is fixed in repeated sampling, then:

$$Var(\hat{\beta}) = (X'X)^{-1} X'E(uu')X(X'X)^{-1}$$

Assuming (B.2) no HK and (B.3) no autocorrelation, then E(uu') = σ^2, so:

$$Var(\hat{\beta}) = (X'X)^{-1} X'\sigma^2 X(X'X)^{-1}$$

$$Var(\hat{\beta}) = \sigma^2 (X'X)^{-1} (X'X)(X'X)^{-1}$$

$$Var(\hat{\beta}) = \sigma^2 (X'X)^{-1}$$

However, if there is AC then $E(uu') \neq \sigma^2 = \Lambda$ so:

$$Var(\hat{\beta}) = (X'X)^{-1} X'\Lambda X(X'X)^{-1}$$

So AC causes t tests to become invalid. Assuming there is positive AC and this is unaccounted for by OLS, then OLS variances are biased downwards, OLS standard errors are biased downwards and thus OLS t stats are biased upwards. So under OLS, there is an increased chance of making a type 1 error, $\hat{\beta}$ may be wrongly concluded to be significant when it is actually insignificant.

www.ingramcontent.com/pod-product-compliance
Lightning Source LLC
Chambersburg PA
CBHW081049170526
45158CB00006B/1913